Nations, States, and Violence

Nations, States, and Violence

DAVID D. LAITIN

OXFORD
UNIVERSITY PRESS

OXFORD

UNIVERSITY PRESS

Great Clarendon Street, Oxford ox2 6DP

Oxford University Press is a department of the University of Oxford.
It furthers the University's objective of excellence in research, scholarship,
and education by publishing worldwide in

Oxford New York

Auckland Cape Town Dar es Salaam Hong Kong Karachi
Kuala Lumpur Madrid Melbourne Mexico City Nairobi
New Delhi Shanghai Taipei Toronto

With offices in

Argentina Austria Brazil Chile Czech Republic France Greece
Guatemala Hungary Italy Japan Poland Portugal Singapore
South Korea Switzerland Thailand Turkey Ukraine Vietnam

Oxford is a registered trade mark of Oxford University Press
in the UK and in certain other countries

Published in the United States
by Oxford University Press Inc., New York

British Library Cataloguing in Publication Data

Data available

Library of Congress Cataloging in Publication Data

Data available

Typeset by SPI Publisher Services, Pondicherry, India
Printed in Great Britain
on acid-free paper by
Biddles Ltd., King's Lynn, Norfolk

ISBN 978–0–19–922823–2

1 3 5 7 9 10 8 6 4 2

This book is dedicated to the memory of Ernst B. Haas, teacher, dissertation adviser, and friend who taught generations of students and colleagues to think about and beyond the nation-state.

PREFACE

Nations, States, and Violence presents a revisionist view of nationalism. It analyzes the relationships of the nation and its cultural underpinnings—to violence, prosperity, and the state.

My revisionist stance begins in Chapter 1, where I challenge the common view that the specter haunting world peace today is that of ethnic or civilizational divides. This popular fear of unleashed nationalism, once the data are examined carefully, is highly exaggerated. In fact, in our world ethnic cooperation is the norm, and the contagion of civil wars in our time is not due to ethnic hatreds. Nonetheless, the dangers to the world presented by the mass killings of ethnic 'others' in Rwanda, Sudan, and Yugoslavia, not to mention the death of some seventeen million people due to civil war violence in the past half-century, demand that we better understand what nationalism and its cultural foundations are all about, when difference is most likely to become lethal, and how to manage cultural and national difference politically.

The next two chapters explore the Janus-facedness of national identities, sailing between the Scylla of the primordialists (who see national identities as the culmination of ancient ethnic attachments) and the Charybdis of the instrumentalists (who see national identities as merely the result of strategic choices for purposes of materialist gain). In opposition to the primordialists, Chapter 2 highlights the first face of culture, in which strategic coordination makes culture seem stable, yet allows for rapid shifts in cultural identification. Nations are both formed and reformed through the processes of strategic coordination described in this chapter.

In opposition to the instrumentalists, Chapter 3 uncovers the cultural foundations of national identities and provides a glimpse of why people find their identities valuable. Here is revealed culture's second face, in which shared symbols are the foundation for common world views, giving members of a cultural group a shared vision of what is worth fighting for.

The Janus-faced images of Chapters 2 and 3 combine to provide an equilibrium theory of culture. Equilibrium theory explains short-term stability, where such things as cultural norms in a group and the ethnic heterogeneity of the population are self-enforcing, meaning that no one has an incentive to deviate from either the norms of their cultural group or membership in it. But a variety of factors—the efforts of ethnic entrepreneurs, the vision of citizens who foresee changed opportunities, and shifts in the external environment—can point to alternative cultural equilibria. Dynamic equilibrium models reveal stability in the short term and the possibility of change in the long term.

These equilibrium ideas are applied in Chapter 4 to analyze the historical relationship of nation and state. Here it is shown why the nation-state, the modal form of sovereign rule in the modern era, may no longer be an equilibrium.

In fact Chapter 4 composes an epitaph for the nation-state as conventionally understood.

Finally, in Chapter 5, a new political formula—the liberal democratic approach to the nation—is offered as a way to accrue the benefits of national/cultural revivals without incurring too much the cost in loss of social solidarity, or the disruption from changed state boundaries, or engendering a process that inflames rather than ameliorates nationalist passions.

This book has the ambition of following in Aristotle's footsteps in a field of politics—culture and nationalism—that was foreign to him. Of the many goals in his *Politics*, one was to grasp why some communities flourished in peace while others fell into violent conflict. He examined 154 polities to demonstrate that regime-type affects both community performance and persistence. His empirical investigations suggested practical measures that would help stabilize existing states. Empirics served as a foundation for his normative justifications for constitutions that were successful in enhancing justice and stability.

The normative conclusion reached here, one that follows an empirical course not unlike Aristotle's, is that multiculturalism has value and properly promoted can work better than it has in the past. However, it is acknowledged that the costs of promoting multiculturalism are nontrivial. The book before you, then, due to the foregrounding of the trade-offs involved in both promoting and containing nationalism, is marred by the guarded complexity that has frustrated generations of would-be Aristotelians. But the hard reality reveals that here is no national state of our prayers.

There are two origins to the chapters in this book. First, they represent an integration of work I have been doing for most of my career, based on fieldwork in Somalia, Nigeria, Spain, and Estonia. From these field experiences, I have published work for scholarly audiences. I see in this book an opportunity to bring together a variety of articles and books to offer an original and coherent approach to the study of nationalism and its political and economic implications.

Second, these chapters are developments of three lectures I gave in Taiwan compliments of the Shih Mingteh Lecture Foundation at the National Taiwan University. There, I was treated royally, but also got an appreciation for the excitement some of my interpretations held for nonspecialists. The reception received to these lectures in Taiwan served as a motivation to publish revised versions of them in the book before you.

Thanks go to my many collaborators over the years— Rogers Brubaker, Kanchan Chandra, James Fearon, Avner Greif, Rob Reich, and Barry Weingast—whose joint formulations with me appear throughout these chapters. These collaborators, from our co-authored work and from their critical readings of my manuscripts, including this one, have taught me much about the world, and even more about my own perspective on it. After I drafted my lectures and revised them into a book manuscript Joshua Cohen, Henry Frisch, Jack Goldstone, Peter Katzenstein, Ira Katznelson, Yotam Margalit, and Sidney Tarrow read what I sent them and pushed me further for elaboration and clarity. I then subjected myself to the brutal criticisms of the Comparative Politics Workshop at Stanford

University. I want especially to thank David Abernethy, Claire Adida, Leonardo Arriola, Luke Condra, Ebru Erdem, Suraj Jacob, Bethany Lacina, Josiah Ober, Maggie Peters, Natan Sachs, and Jeremy Weinstein for their unrelenting criticisms both at the workshop session and in subsequent correspondence.

CONTENTS

Figures and Table   xv

1 The Pandemonium of Nations   1
2 National Cascades   29
3 The Cultural Foundations of Nationalism   61
4 Nations and the Twenty-First Century State   81
5 Managing the Multinational State   107

Notes   139
References to Author's Own Work   153
Index   157

FIGURES AND TABLE

Figure 1.1. Ethnic diversity, country wealth, and
   civil war probability   14
Figure 2.1. De Swaan's floral model   33
Figure 2.2. Tipping game for minorities   38
Figure 2.3. Tipping game for marginals   50
Figure 3.1. Somali and English dialogues on
   authority claims   73
Figure 3.2. Somali and English dialogues on
   substantive claims   73

Table 1.1. Horowitz's theory of ethnic secessions
   applied to post-Soviet cases   17

CHAPTER 1

The Pandemonium
of Nations

'Nation states no longer seem inclined to go to war
with one another, but ethnic groups fight all the time.'

Daniel P. Moynihan in *Pandaemonium:
Ethnicity in International Politics*

IS nationalism dangerous? Among the educated public
and social scientists, this question appears naive. Of
course it is. Nationalism, they will point out, is a relatively
modern phenomenon, but it has already made its mark in
the history of violent conflict. Napoleon demonstrated to
the world that conscripted soldiers fighting for their nation
will fight more fiercely for far lower pay than mercenary
armies. It was a bullet from the gun of a Serbian nationalist
that set off the chain of events leading to World War I
in 1914. Two principal motives of Hitler in fighting what
became World War II were to recover national honor and
to purify his nation by murdering non-Aryans. And in
the world in the past half-century, numerous civil wars—
the Algerians against the French, the Biafrans against
the Nigerians, the Acehnese against the Indonesians, the

Basques against the Spaniards, and the Tibetans against the Chinese, just to name a few—were fought in the name of national liberation. Of course, conventional wisdom has it, nationalism is dangerous. Books entitled *The Clash of Civilizations, Containing Nationalism*, and *Modern Hatreds: the Symbolic Politics of Ethnic War* attest to the assumption of nationalist danger.[1]

The historical record identifies many routes from ethnicity or nationalism to violence—and I shall guide readers through these routes in the following pages. Readers will be left with an initial impression that the conventional wisdom is correct. But a more systematic examination of that record—one that follows—will reveal the supposed affinity of national difference and violence to be a chimera. We then need to explore why our popular impressions are so wrong-headed so that we can put former United Nations Ambassador Daniel Moynihan's portrayal of pandemonium to rest.

MECHANISMS LINKING NATIONALISM AND VIOLENCE

There are four routes leading national and ethnic groups to violence either against their state or against ethnic/national others: irredentism, secession, sons-of-the-soil, and communalism. The first three routes—as well as a mixed category that will be referred to as the triadic configuration—are justified by challengers to the status quo with a view that all nations merit their own states. State leaders, using mirror-image arguments for their efforts to make national boundaries commensurate with state boundaries, stress 'purity'. The ultimate logic of such claims has genocidal implications, as were seen with the 'impure' Jews and Gypsies in Germany, the Armenians in the Ottoman Empire, the Tutsis in Rwanda, and the Albanians in Serbia.

Irredentism

Interstate violence has followed when a nation has a state of its own but seeks to redeem territory occupied by fellow nationals living in a neighboring state. This mechanism took on the name of *irredenta* ('unredeemed' in Italian) when after the uniting of modern Italy, its nationalists sought to incorporate the Austrian possessions of Trentino, Trieste, Dalmatia, Istria, South Tyrol, Gorizia, Ticino, Nice, Corsica, and Malta. Italy's entry into World War I was based on a promise through a pact signed in London that after Austria's defeat, Italy would receive some of these territories. Germany initiated the hostilities that led to World War II by making irredentist claims to the Sudetenland, populated by Germans but under Czechoslovak administration. In the post-World War II era, the Somalis, divided into five administrative areas in the colonial period, got their own state in 1960, with only two of the territories under Somali state rule. Kenya's Northeastern Province, France's Territory of Afars and Issas, and the Ethiopian Ogaadeen region remained under separate administration. The new Somali government designed a flag with a five-pointed star symbolizing the national goal to incorporate their three unredeemed territories. In the early 1960s, it sponsored guerrilla bands in Kenya seeking to redeem Kenya's

Northeastern Province, and in 1977 its armies invaded Ethiopia in the hope of redeeming the Ogaadeen.

Secession

Intrastate violence has followed from the inverse of the irredentist issue—here when a nation is not larger but rather smaller than the state, and its self-appointed representatives seek to have a state of their own. Ernest Gellner, the doyen of nationalist theory in the past century, mapped this route with analytic precision, postulating an industrial core (which he calls Megalomania) and a rural backwater (which he calls Ruritania). Ruritanian workers migrate to the industrial core of their state, but because of their identifiable characteristics as foreigners, they face discrimination as they seek social mobility beyond their positions in manual labor. Frustrated by their lack of inclusion in Megalomanian high society, they return to Ruritania declaring that their identifiable differences amount to national differences and demanding a state of their own. If Megalomania resists the diminishing of its historical state boundaries, a Ruritanian resistance will challenge those boundaries in a guerrilla war.[2]

Secessionist movements with this storyline are ubiquitous, even if Gellner's is not the only mechanism that has driven nationalist entrepreneurs into the politics of secession. In the name of their nation, the South Slavs sought their own state separate from the Austro-Hungarian Empire, the Irish sought separation from Britain, the Basques sought separation from Spain, the Igbos (as Biafrans) sought separation from Nigeria, the Acehnese and the Timorians have sought separation from Indonesia, and the Tamils have sought separation from Sri Lanka. All of these separatist movements were resisted by the megalomaniacal state and were followed by violent warfare. The prevalence of these civil wars has certainly helped reinforce beliefs that nationalism is indeed dangerous.

Irredentism Combined with Secession

Irredentism combined with secession—what Rogers Brubaker calls the triadic configuration—is especially dangerous. Here we have three actors—national minorities, nationalizing states, and external national homelands. Consider the German national minority in the interwar Czechoslovak Republic (a nationalizing state favoring its Czech and Slovak citizens), with Germany as the external national homeland interested in the fate of the German minority. Hitler exploited this conflict and used it as a justification for the German invasion of the Sudetenland. In this same interwar era, Hungary (the external national homeland) demanded rights for Hungarians (the national minority) in Romania (the nationalizing state) in response to the (from the Hungarian point of view, historically tragic) Treaty of Trianon (1920) that awarded the largely Hungarian-populated region of Transylvania to Romania. Although this did not lead to war, it has many times brought Hungary and Romania to its brink.[3]

This triadic configuration reproduced itself with the collapses of the Soviet Union and Yugoslavia. Serbia as the external national homeland for Serbs helped incite the Serbs in the Krajina region of Croatia and the Serbian area of Bosnia into violent rebellion against their new nationalizing states. Armenia as the external national homeland for Armenians helped incite the Armenian minority in Azerbaijan's Nagorno Karabakh into rebellion. Russia (or at least its 14th Army)—the external national homeland for diasporic Russians from the Soviet era—helped incite the Slavic population in Transdniestria into rebellion against the nationalizing state of Moldova.

Sons-of-the-Soil

Sons-of-the-soil movements have been violent and also reflect national conflicts.[4] Consider a state whose dominant population lives in an overpopulated core zone of the country, with a minority population in an impoverished dry zone in the periphery. With support from the World Bank or other international donors, the state invests heavily in dams and irrigation schemes to enrich the soil of the formerly dry zone. With new agricultural opportunities, the state wins support from its core constituency by inducing them to migrate as homesteaders in the newly irrigated lands. These migrations induce resentment by the indigenous populations of the region; but when the demographic balance in the dry region shifts in favor of the dominant nationality group of the country, the indigenous population sees this as a loss of their historic homeland. This drives the outraged (and often displaced) minority into the hills as guerrilla bands organized to reclaim their homeland.

Indigenous populations organized 'sons-of-the-soil' attacks on American westward expansion in the nineteenth century. The irrigation schemes in the northeastern province of Sri Lanka set off a sons-of-the-soil rebellion that followed this same script. Other cases of sons-of-the-soil insurgencies (with their distinct sources for induced migration) include the Chakma peoples in the Chitttagong Hills of Bangladesh, the Nagas and other 'tribals' in northeast India, the Moros in the Philippines, the Uighurs in Xinjiang province in China, a variety of ethnic minorities in Burma, the Sindhis against the Mohajirs around Karachi in Pakistan, the Bougainvilleans in Papua New Guinea, both the West Papuans and Acehnese in Indonesia, and the Tuaregs in Mali.

Pogroms and Communal Warfare

A final form of ethnic/national violence is communal, when (quasi-)organized militias of one ethnic group attack civilians (in which the attacks are called 'pogroms') and/or militias (in which the attacks and counterattacks are called 'communal warfare') from another ethnic group that is living in the same place. In these cases the state might be an instigator, a passive observer that supports the attackers by not sending in the police to cauterize the violence, or a third party seeking to negotiate a truce. Pogroms against Jews in Russia's Pale of Settlement, against Armenians in the Ottoman Empire as a prelude to the genocide, against (then-called) Negroes in the American South, against Muslims in North India, and against Chinese in Indonesia are well-known examples of this form of ethnic/nationalist violence.

An oft-cited explanation for pogroms implicates job competition in an urban environment.[5] Workers occupying a certain niche in the division of labor in a society under conditions of labor shortage have advantages in pressing for wage increases. When new groups enter the niche (e.g. as in Susan Olzak's study, African-Americans free to move from the south to northern cities in the USA), they threaten the wage security of the older working class. If the new workers are marked ethnically, resentment of them by entrenched workers will induce those workers to intimidate the migrants, which in the US case meant lynching. To be sure, there is a range of other mechanisms that drive ethnic difference into localized violence, but many of them boil down to issues involving economic competition.[6]

Communal warfare is less asymmetric than pogroms, but like pogroms, it takes place without the state army fighting on one side. Such warfare has taken place between Nuers and Dinkas in Sudan, Kalenjins and Maasai in Kenya, Africans and Arabs in Darfur as well as in Senegal, Abgals and Habr Gedirs in Somalia, Ijaws and Itsekiris in Nigeria, and Shi'ites and Sunnis in Iraq in the wake of the American-led invasion. Reports on these wars typically report on ancient and even modern hatreds that turn into violence when despised groups seek vengeance against their oppressors, in what Horowitz calls the 'struggle for relative group worth'.[7]

Hindu–Muslim riots in India stand somewhere in between pogroms and communal warfare. Numerous studies analyze these events across North India, in large part because of the hundreds of thousands of lives lost in the violence associated with the Indian partition in 1947 that created a separate Muslim state (Pakistan) but left millions of Muslims in Hindu-dominant India. Why has this brutal communalism continued for a half-century? Some scholars point to the historic injustices of the British *raj* along with its divide-and-rule strategy to maintain order.[8] Others point to the lack of cross-cutting cleavages among the two religious groups, such that there were hardly any associations that included Muslims and Hindus that would have had an interest in cauterizing violent assaults on poor Muslims by what Brass calls Hindu 'riot entrepreneurs'. Recent work points to a different mechanism—namely the fear of politicians representing well-to-do Hindu voters of an electoral alliance between poor Hindus and Muslims that would defeat the upper caste Hindus who remain at the core of the Indian ruling classes. To forestall such an alliance, these politicians seed riots whose goal is to convince poor Hindus that there can never be a trusting relationship with Muslim groups. In this example, pogroms are an element of an electoral strategy.[9]

Ancient hatreds, cultural resentment, economic niches, and electoral advantage are some of the leading candidates to explain the kind of communal violence that seems nearly a natural component of our social lives.

THE DATA

If we change our perspective from one that asks for a catalogue of ethnic conflicts that have led to violence to one that asks about the probability of violence given ethnic difference, the world takes on a very different color. Quantitative analyses that ask about probabilities lead us to view ethnic violence as rare, and ethnic difference as unimportant for the explanation of communal conflict and contemporary civil war onsets. Let us now look at the data.

In-Group Policing and Interethnic Cooperation

The opening page of Horowitz's seminal work on ethnic conflict provides a gruesome list of the world's trouble zones, thereby providing, in his judgment, 'abundant... evidence [that] ethnic conflict is a worldwide phenomenon'. This study has set the agenda for the past twenty years in seeking its causes and attempting remedies. As noted earlier, this view has become a common wisdom, articulated by Ambassador Moynihan and quoted as the epigraph for this chapter.

A list of illustrative cases, however, does not constitute systematic evidence. Consider Africa, a continent that many have described as especially prone to communal conflicts. A computation of estimates of communal violence— 'an event of short duration... in which two identifiable communal groups are antagonists in violence to secure some short-term goal'—was compiled from a data-set that spanned from 1960 through 1979.[10] To avoid selection bias—that is, only looking at cases where violence took place—actual cases were compared to potential cases per year. The potential cases per country and year were a conservative estimate of the number of ethnic neighbors in regular interaction in each African country, computed to be 38,383 across the continent. The data-set records twenty incidents of communal violence in this period. A catalogue and lurid description of these episodes would leave the impression, as it did to Ambassador Moynihan, of a bloody continent. However, the percentage of neighboring ethnic groups that experienced violent communal incidents was infinitesimal—for any randomly chosen but neighboring pair of ethnic groups, on average only 5 in 10,000 had a recorded violent conflict in any year. From these data, it could be concluded that communal violence in Africa has been, in fact, very rare!

Even in the best-known cases of communal violence, the image of ethnic groups at each other's throats is a vast misrepresentation. Take for example Hindu–Muslim violence in India since 1950, an exemplary case of the phenomenon to be explained. In a data-set compiled by Ashutosh Varshney and Steven Wilkinson, they find that in the period from 1950 to 1995, communal violence accounted for some 10,000 deaths. This is horrific, but it hardly evokes the image of pandemonium. The deaths amount to about one-fiftieth on an annual per capita basis compared to Northern Ireland which is a danger-ous place, but hardly a zone of killing fields. Not only is the aggregate figure limited, but also the distribution of the violence is also quite narrow. Rural India, where two-thirds of all Indians lived in the period covered by the data-set, accounted for less than 4 percent of deaths from communal violence. Furthermore, within the urban areas, 8 cities representing 18 percent of urban India accounted for nearly half of the deaths. In religiously heterogeneous rural areas and in the majority of religiously heterogeneous cities, there has been almost no communal violence.[11]

The real challenge for understanding communal rela-tions, given the vast potential for violence, is the near ubiquity of ethnic cooperation. Ambassador Moynihan got the story backwards—*people belonging to different ethnic groups cooperate nearly all the time.*

Ethnic Linguistic Fractionalization and Civil War

Rather than enumerate the cases in which ethnic difference drove parties into large-scale violence, it is preferable to put together a data-set of all country years and to ask what differentiates observations in which there was a civil war onset from those in which there was no onset. This data-set will tell us whether knowledge of the ethnic/national configuration in any country is helpful in making such a differentiation.

By ethnic/national configuration, political scientists have relied on a dispersion index, computed with the equation below (called in the literature Ethnic Linguistic Fractionalization, or ELF). This formula, by computing the sum of the squares of each group's share of the population and then subtracting that figure from one, reveals the probability that two randomly matched people in the country will be of different ethnic groups. In Sri Lanka, according to the *CIA Factbook*, the Sinhalese make up 73.8 percent of the population, the Moors 7.2 percent, the (combined Sri Lankan and Indian) Tamils 8.5 percent, and 10.5 percent are unspecified or other. Its ELF score is 0.42 percent, meaning that if any two Sri Lankans were randomly paired, there would be a 42 percent chance that they were from different ethnic communities. But compare this to Kazakhstan. The *CIA World Factbook* reports that Kazakhs make up 53.4 percent of the population, Russians 30 percent, Ukrainians 3.7 percent, Uzbeks 2.5 percent, Germans 2.4 percent, Tatars 1.7 percent, Uyghurs 1.4 percent, and others 4.9 percent. The ELF score computes to a 61 percent chance that two residents of Kazakhstan randomly paired will come from a different ethnic group, making it far more fractionalized than Sri Lanka.

$$\text{ELF} = 1 - \sum_{i=1}^{n} p_i^2$$

Other algorithms square the ELF figure, with the notion that homogeneous and heterogeneous countries are both less susceptible to ethnic war than countries that have moderate levels of heterogeneity. Some suggest that it is the size of the plurality ethnic group that matters, with the idea that the smaller the plurality group, the more likely it is to be challenged by the second largest group. I invite readers to consult the *CIA Factbook* to compute the ELF for any country in the world.[12]

With a data-set spanning 1945–99 including all countries in the world above a minimum population for all years that they have been independent, we can ask whether any specification of ethnic fractionalization, controlling for country wealth and other factors, could help determine which countries would be most susceptible to a civil war onset.[13] The answer is plain: knowing the degree of ethnic fractionalization (or its square) is not helpful (i.e. not statistically significant) in being able to differentiate country/years with civil war onsets from those country/years without civil war onsets. The albeit arbitrary illustration of the ELF scores for Sri Lanka and Kazakhstan illustrates this finding. It is the less-fractionalized country (Sri Lanka) that has experienced three civil wars,[14] and the more fractionalized country (Kazakhstan) none. To be sure, if ELF is squared, Sri Lanka would be scored as more susceptible to

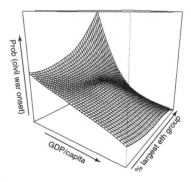

Figure 1.1. Ethnic diversity, country wealth, and civil war probability

a civil war onset relative to Kazakhstan. But the general relationship of ELF-squared to civil war onset remains insignificant.

A neat way to view the results is presented on a landscape portrayed in Figure 1.1. Going from left to right, the wealth of the country (measured by GDP/cap) goes up. Going from bottom to top, the probability of a civil war increases. Going from front to back, the homogeneity of the society (measured now by the percentage in the country of the largest ethnic group) increases. At low levels of wealth (on the far left of the figure), defying the conventional wisdom about ELF, as cultural homogeneity increases, so does the probability of a civil war onset. But at the highest levels of country wealth (on the far right of the figure), now in accord with the conventional wisdom, an increase in homogeneity lowers the probability of a civil war onset. At the middle levels of country wealth, an increase in cultural homogeneity first increases and then decreases the probability of a civil war onset. The figure nicely shows a landscape in which the probability of a civil war onset rises and falls in no consistent pattern with the ethnic configuration.

Looking at the complete data-set of civil war onsets reveals cases such as Somalia (with high levels of homogeneity in ELF but with two civil wars) and Tanzania (with incredible heterogeneity and no civil war). There are also cases with a plurality group and a significant minority (where ELF-squared is high) such as Canada and Estonia with no civil wars. In sum, there is no consistent relationship between ethnic demography and the likelihood of a civil war.

Hatreds and Civil War

The notion that ethnic war is the result of ethnic resentment or even hatred seems so obvious that it has rarely been tested. But in a study of war and peace in six post-Soviet states, these notions were put to test.[15] Each of these post-Soviet republics had significant minorities that had reason to believe that they would face domination by the national group that purportedly owned the state (called 'titulars' in the Soviet world). Four of them had peaceful transitions without civil war: Estonia, Latvia, Ukraine, and Kazakhstan. Two of them experienced civil wars: Moldova and Azerbaijan.

Surprisingly, the study revealed no relationship between measures of hatred or resentment during the Soviet period and post-Soviet rebellions by minority groups. To elaborate on these findings, let us begin with the relationship of ethnic resentment and its motivation for political secession. Horowitz's resentment theory argues that backward groups in economically disadvantaged regions have the greatest level of resentment and therefore the highest motivation to seek secession, and to do so early. This is because backward groups in backward regions have the greatest need for the restoration of self-esteem, and they are consequently willing to pay the highest costs at the earliest moment to regain it through owning a state. With this theory in mind, the data presented on Table 1.1 show that of the six ethnic minorities in post-Soviet states in the republics under consideration, the theory makes two correct and four incorrect predictions. The Armenians in Azerbaijan and the Slavs in Moldova were not lacking in self-esteem, yet these were the two cases of rebellion. Meanwhile, the two relatively backward groups whose members felt great resentment for their backwardness (the Russians in Estonia and the Gagauz in Moldova) were angry but did not mobilize militias to challenge their states militarily in order to secede. While the theory correctly predicted no rebellion in two cases—that of the Russians in Ukraine and Kazakhstan—a theory with such a poor success ratio is suspect.

What about hatreds? It is not possible to measure comparative hatreds directly—after all, how can we know if Serbs hated Bosniaks more than Estonians hated Russians without biasing our results by looking at who actually fought? However, indirectly we can say that the greater the levels of social contact between members of different groups, the less likely these groups hold each other in contempt. Survey data I collected with Jerry Hough for the four peaceful republics and supplemented later with evidence from the two republics that experienced civil war violence reveal no significant differences in the

Table 1.1. Horowitz's theory of ethnic secessions applied to post-Soviet cases

Group/Country	Group Status	Regional Status	Horowitz prediction for secession	Secessionist Outcome
Slavs/Moldova	Advanced	Advanced	Late, rare	Early
Armenians/Azerbaijan	Advanced	Backward	Late, frequent	Early
Gagauz/Moldova	Backward	Backward	Early, frequent	No secession (though a near miss)
Russians/Estonia	Backward	Backward	Early, frequent	No secession
Russians/Latvia	Backward	Not regionally concentrated	No prediction	No secession
Russians/Kazakhstan	Advanced	Advanced	Late, rare	No secession
Russians/Ukraine	Advanced	Advanced	Late, rare	No secession

social relations between minorities and the titulars in the late Soviet period. There is little difference, for example, in the rates that minorities learned the titular language. Furthermore, the violent minorities in Moldova and Azerbaijan had higher scores on an index called 'openness to assimilation' than the average for all Soviet republics. This index measures respondents' acceptance of their children marrying outside their ethnic group, their views about the use of the titular language in public places, and their reactions to government officials addressing them in the titular language. In the cases of Slavs (in Moldova) and Armenians (from Azerbaijan, but surveyed in refugee status)—the two cases of rebellion—most respondents (before the wars began) thought it natural that their children should have an educational foundation in the titular language of their republic and that it would be fine if their children married into the titular community. It would consequently be impossible from these surveys to pick out Moldova and Azerbaijan as republics that were on the brink of war at the time of the Soviet collapse due to the opportunity to settle scores with the hated ethnic 'other'.[16]

In summary, the post-Soviet world was rife with resentment and even hatred! But there is no demonstrated relationship of the level of these emotions and the probability of a civil war onset.

Group Concentration and Ethnic Violence (Sons-of-the-Soil)

The Minorities at Risk data-set is the most complete catalogue of minority (and most of them ethnic) groups throughout the world since 1945.[17] Hundreds of groups that are judged to lack physical security were identified. Variables were created measuring each group's size, its distribution throughout the country, its political, economic, and cultural rights, and many other factors on their standing within their country. There is also systematic information on their levels of rebellion against the state. Analysis of these data reveals, as with the data-set described earlier, that cultural differences between minorities and the dominant cultural group of their state measured in a variety of ways do not help distinguish groups that have been in rebellion from those that have not. Nor do economic differentials. Nor do levels of social and political discrimination, for example in regard to legislation against the use of regional languages. Most of the significant 'predictors' of rebellion, as is discussed in the conclusion of this chapter, are based on country-level factors that have little to do with ethnicity or nationalism.

Territorial concentration of groups, however, is associated with civil war violence. The more that groups are settled in a single region of the country, the more likely they will be in rebellion against the state. Geographically peripheral ethnic groups that seek to forestall the taking of jobs and land in their region by interlopers from the dominant group typically see themselves as 'sons-of-the-soil'. It has been suggested that group identification with a territory and group fears that its sacred land will be occupied by people of the dominant cultural group is what drives peripheral minorities into rebellion.[18] If the state is engaged in 'nation-building'—that is, the policy to make the boundaries of the state commensurate with the boundaries of the nation—and does so by seeking to affect the cultural composition of peripheral regions, and if this policy provokes the peoples of peripheral regions into civil war, then we can say that in this case, nationalism is dangerous.

But what distinguishes territorial grievances from other grievances such as language, economic opportunity, and religion that are not statistically associated with rebellion? An analysis of the Tamil rebellion in Sri Lanka, which had both a linguistic and a sons-of-the-soil grievance, provides a preliminary answer. When the Sinhala-led government (following what the British did as colonial rulers) further opened up the Tamil-majority dry lands to irrigation, it was able to facilitate a large-scale homesteading migration by land-hungry Sinhalese peasants from the south central zone of the country. As these peasants-turned-yeoman-farmers settled in Tamil areas, there ensued the kind of everyday ethnically colored gang violence typical of urban centers everywhere. But in the northeast of Sri Lanka, with the police dominated by Tamils recruited locally, Sinhala migrants could not get protection from vandalism and other threats to their security during bouts of violence. They appealed to the central state for protection, and the government responded with plans to build military bases in the region that would serve as the foundation for civic order. The government then sent military convoys up the eastern coast of the island, into areas that were foreign to most soldiers. These convoys were easily vulnerable to ambush by angry Tamil gangs who could after their attacks surreptitiously escape into the inland forest areas. The military, lacking information on who was culpable, bombed inland villages in retribution. These attacks killed more innocents than guilty, and incentivized formerly peaceful Tamils to join an emerging resistance movement. Escalation of violence on both sides continued, and this series of actions and reactions was an important mechanism leading to the civil war beginning in 1983, and killing as many as 60,000 people up to today.

Sons-of-the-soil movements are not uncommon. But the suggestion here is that what drives them into violent confrontations with the state has less to do with nationalist yearnings for control over historical territory than the inability of the state to provide security for their home-steaders in the region of settlement, and its inability to accurately target sons-of-the-soil insurgents.

The Sources of Civil War Violence Today

What have we learned from the systematic examination of complete and therefore unbiased data? First, the case against heterogeneity that assumes a relationship between ethnic difference and violence rests on a weak foundation. Second, we need to look elsewhere for the sources of contemporary civil war. The culprit is the weak state, unable to provide basic services to its population, unable to police its peripheries, and unable to distinguish law abiders from lawbreakers.[19] Indicators of weak states— when their institutions are unproven such as when they are newly independent or newly democratizing or sud-denly becoming more authoritarian—are good predictors of civil war. And ecological conditions, such as moun-tainous terrain (making states weak in regard to weeding out insurgents), are also associated with civil war onsets. Under these conditions, civil war is profitable for potential insurgents, in that they can both survive and enjoy some probability of winning the state. If there is an economic motive for civil war in the past half-century, it is in the expectation of collecting the revenues that ownership of the state avails, and thus the statistical association between oil (which provides unimaginably high rents to owners of states) and civil war.[20]

In the name of nationalism, insurgents have taken advantage of state incompetence. Furthermore, weakly institutionalized states cannot commit to minorities that any concessions given to them will still be honored when the state (re)gains its ability to project power. This is the source of the commitment problem—'we historically forgotten people are being offered crumbs by a crumbling state, but even those crumbs will be taken from us as soon as the state regains capacity to destroy us'—that fuels nationalist rhetoric.[21]

The popular belief that nationalism and ethnic differences in and of themselves are dangerous is discredited by quantitative research. Immunity from civil violence comes with building states with the power and the incentive to enforce the rule of law. Weak, incompetent states unable to enforce the rule of law are dangerous.

WHY DO ACCUMULATED WISDOM AND DATA CONFLICT?

This chapter first pointed to a conventional wisdom that nationalism is dangerous. Indeed, the historical and contemporary evidence showing links between nationalism and violence is impressive. Quantitative data, however, undermine confidence in theories purporting to show that national aspirations, differences, or demographies are systematically associated with communal violence or civil war. What explains this disconnect?

Selection bias is one culprit. Consider the following two controlled comparisons: that between regional separatist movements in Basque Country (a high violence case) and Catalonia (a low violence case) in Spain since 1975; and that between postindependence challenges to the new states of the former Soviet Union in Georgia (a high violence case) and Ukraine (a low violence case).[22] In the literature on these historical examples, far more attention was given to the violent cases than the peaceful ones. This reflects a bias in the literature on nationalism, one that overemphasizes explanations for violence at the expense of explanations for peace. Indeed, the academic and journalistic literature focuses attention far more on the few cases of communal violence than on the normal situation of ethnic peace.

This suggests a second culprit—that of listening too earnestly to the accounts of combatants. When ethnic war breaks out, journalists congregate like ravens. They inevitably ask combatants to tell narratives explaining the killing. The combatants are trying to answer the same question for themselves! It makes sense to link the fighting to historical experiences of grievance for two reasons. First, the leaders of a rebellion need to get support for their insurgencies. During the Cold War, they could call themselves communists to get support from the Soviet Union or free marketeers to get support from the USA. But as the Cold War waned, these appeals fell flat. Meanwhile appeals to ethnic diasporas about historical grievances and showing videos of the horrors of counterinsurgency tactics tended to be more successful, and thus copied by other insurgent leaders. Linking an insurgency to a nationalist cause helps to sustain that insurgency. This is not the same as causing the insurgency, as the historical grievances that are appealed to by insurgents are ubiquitous, and not any greater in cases of insurgency than in cases of peace. The images of brethren tortured and killed are, of course, powerful, but again they are the result of—used as proof of the need for autonomy—but not the cause of the insurgency.

To show how selection of cases to observe and listening too closely to the narratives of combatants bias our understanding, consider the 1991 rebellion in the Transdniestrian region of Moldova, fought between the Moldovan state and a separatist region. Journalists flocked to this former Soviet Republic to report on this war. Many of the insurgents complained bitterly that Moldova's language laws discriminated against the Russian-speaking populations in the Transdniestrian zone. Journalists gave these stories causal weight. But Russian-speakers in Estonia's northeastern region were equally disgruntled while voting for national separatism in 1991. Journalists flocked to Narva, the center of anti-Estonian opposition. But when the specter of violence receded, so did the journalists. Without a war, they did not have notebooks filled with Russian-speakers' testimonies about their grievances. In sum, people caught in the throes of a civil war fought in their name are trying to make sense of the war; they are not, as too many journalists imply, making causal claims.

Can it possibly be the case that the expressed grievances revealed to journalists play no role in the choice of violent confrontation with authority? Quite the contrary. Grievances are relevant; in fact, they are usually motivating factors for violent mobilization. But ethnic grievances are commonly felt and latent; the factors that make these grievances vital and manifest differentiate the violent from the nonviolent cases. *Ex ante* measures of grievance levels are not good predictors of the transformation of latent grievances into manifest ones. And it is the factors that turn latent grievances into violent action that should be considered as explanatory for that violence.

Listening too earnestly to the narratives of the combatants has a related bias. Secessionist or autonomist movements in the name of nationalism—the Basques in Spain, southerners in Sudan, the Irish in UK, the Igbos in Nigeria—invariably threaten the futures of assimilators—that is, those people who are identified by separatist organizations as members of the nationality at risk but who had long beforehand come to terms with the social and political life of the country in which they are an ethnic minority. These people are unenthusiastic about the secessionist project—one that involves *inter alia* sending their children to minority language schools and paying a tax to support guerrilla operations fighting in their name. These people are identified by militant nationalist groups as traitors, and serve as targets for violent revenge. Combatants in national secessionist movements rarely advertise the violence employed to achieve a unity of vision among the minority whom these combatants purport to represent. Yet data from Sri Lanka, Ireland, and southern Sudan show that intra-group killing constitutes a significant percentage of civil war deaths. We learn less about this violence from the manifestos of the organizations fighting secessionist wars, and if we knew more about it, the clarity of our vision of the special ferocity of interethnic violence would become blurred.[23]

There is a third culprit. The way we think about ethnicity and nationalism—namely, that they are built on a rock-solid 'primordial' foundation—makes these attachments seem a threat to the give and take of democratic life. Primordial identities are seen as those given to us by our ancestral links—ethnic and national attachments are seen as hardwired and unyielding. Class differences, in contrast to ethnic differences, permit social mobility, thereby allowing working class youths to envisage themselves as professional class adults. This possibility sets the stage for class compromise. Meanwhile ethnic difference persists, and bargaining between ethnic groups has a zero-sum feel to it.[24] This view gains great support given the ghastly descriptions of pogroms and communal wars that dominate media reports of international events.

Nonetheless, this primordialist vision of ethnicity and nationalism is fundamentally misguided, and it sustains our biased observations on the dangers of ethnic difference. In the next two chapters, I set a new foundation for our understanding of nationalism—where national identities are not given, but in the context of coordination opportunities, are taken; where national cultures are not all-encompassing frameworks but rather sources for useful coordination. From this new viewpoint, we can see the positive possibilities of national/cultural movements rather than fearing them as kindling for civil war fires.

CHAPTER 2

National Cascades

'L'existence d'une nation est (pardonnez-moi cette métaphore) un plébiscite de tous les jours, comme l'existence de l'individu est une affirmation perpétuelle de vie.'

Qu'est-ce qu'une nation? par Ernest Renan;
Conférence faite en Sorbonne, le 11 mars 1882.

HOW are nations formed? Ernest Renan's brilliant lecture over a century ago disputed the accepted wisdom—today called the primordial view—that nations were somehow natural, based on common race, religion, language, or geographical zone. He provided exceptions to every equation linking common culture to the boundaries of the then-existing nations. In its stead, he presented a theory of national consciousness that was constructed on a foundation of collective memories of past glories and collective forgetting of past defeats and internecine massacres. His lecture challenged the German romantics who saw nationhood as a historical fulfillment of a people's destiny. And it challenged as well future projects, such as those of Woodrow Wilson and Joseph Stalin, to find objective criteria for the cultural limits of state boundaries.

Renan's powerful point was that cultures are not given to people by nature, but rather are constructed through collective action and reinforced through the manipulation of collective consciousness.[25]

Those memories and amnesias that form the collective consciousness are, for Renan, aggregated in a metaphoric plebiscite that determines how a people conceive of the size and the cultural content of their nation. By the concept of plebiscite, Renan suggested that people do not inherit their national myths; rather, they choose them, more or less by majority vote. Each citizen becomes a member of the nation that wins the local plebiscite. Thus for Renan, now to use J.-J. Rousseau's terms, a nation is not a biological inheritance but the manifestation of the sum of individual wills or the 'will of all'.

Renan was half right. Nations are indeed the result of the choices made by their prospective members. But these choices, to use the language of modern game theory, are interdependent. Individuals do not choose (or vote in the plebiscite) as with an Australian ballot in absolute privacy. Rather, individual a chooses in large part based on signals received from individuals b, c, d, ..., n on how they will choose; and, of course, these others are looking to a for a signal on how he will choose. Unlike a plebiscite where individuals expect a *division* of votes in their community, when it comes to national identification individuals expect a *coordinated outcome*. And unlike a plebiscite in which different subgroups in a community may have different interests, in the case of national identification, each individual voter gets higher rewards the greater the agreement on a national identity. In the case of nationalism, then,

Rousseau's 'general will'—something greater than the sum of individual wills—is the applicable goal. But how can disparate individuals agree on the general will? Rousseau did not address this problem in *The Social Contract* nor did Renan in his lecture on the nation as a manifestation of the general will, but I will address it now.

TWO MODELS OF INTERDEPENDENT NATIONAL CHOICE

National identities are elusive and consequently hard to measure. Renan was necessarily metaphoric when he spoke of a daily plebiscite, since it is hard to imagine people voting on their national identities. To trace changes in national identity, we need a way to measure it. For this purpose, and with some of the trade-offs for doing so to be discussed in the appendix to this chapter, language will serve as a proxy for national identity, and for several reasons. For one, 'mother tongue' is clearly central to our notion of national membership. Second, language repertoires of individuals—the actual languages they speak—are observable, whereas national identities have no obvious empirical referents. And third, the 'general will' aspect of language is glaringly clear. If within the boundaries of a single country, individual a chooses to learn Swedish, but $b, c, d, \ldots, n$ choose Russian, a is a loser, as he will have no one with whom to communicate. But if a switched to learn Russian, not only would he gain, but so would b, $c, d, \ldots, n$. Individual Russian-speakers do not lose but rather gain when Russian speaking is the general will or national culture. It is to everyone's benefit to coordinate.

But how is coordination managed in large complex societies? Two models of language shift help provide an answer to this question and show how homogeneous national communities get constructed from heterogeneous foundations.

Abram de Swaan's 'Floral Model'

It was well known to Renan that the boundaries of European states were at the beginning incommensurate with language zones. Britain, France, and Spain—considered by many analysts as natural nation-states—were originally multilingual empires. Meanwhile, the German speech zone was and remains larger than the Prussian and now German states. Historical accounts demonstrate that until the late nineteenth century, a significant proportion of French citizens could not successfully communicate in French.[26] Yet over the course of prolonged nation-building experiences, in France and many other states, a hegemonic language regime—in which all citizens view the national language as their mother tongue—emerged. The question is: how?

Abram de Swaan answers this question with a floral model of communication, as illustrated in Figure 2.1.[27] The stamen constitutes that set of people who speak the language of the political center (in the Spanish example in Figure 2.1, this is Castilian); the petals refer to those people who speak one of several languages of the state's periphery (Catalan, Basque, Galician, and Valencian). The structure of the flower (where the petals hardly overlap each other, but all overlap the stamen) is such that some members of

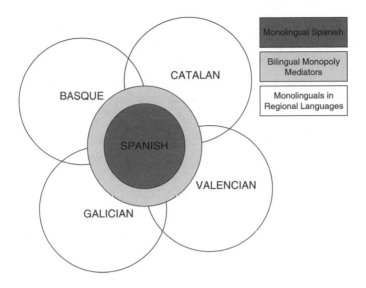

Figure 2.1. De Swaan's floral model

each peripheral group speak the language of the center, but hardly any in the periphery speak the language of another peripheral group. Furthermore, almost no members of the center speak any peripheral language. Under these conditions, de Swaan reckons, there is an incentive for bilingual members of any periphery to serve as *monopoly mediators* between the center and their petal, thereby earning rents through the provision of translation services both to officials in the center (who need to issue orders to and regulate the commercial activities of those in the periphery) and to monolinguals in the periphery (who need at times to petition central authorities for licenses and services of the state). The handsome rewards for providing such services provide an incentive for all those with sufficient resources to invest in bilingual education for their children. When a critical mass of people from the periphery seek either to share in the rents for translation services (lowering the value of the service for each new bilingual) or to avoid paying them through language acquisition, in the long-term all citizens will ultimately 'vote' for education in the central language, ultimately making it hegemonic.

De Swaan's is not a pure coordination game, as there is a conflict of interest inherent in the process. To the extent that all citizens in the periphery learn the language of the center, the monopoly mediators will lose their lucrative roles. Indeed, de Swaan records that these mediators (who wanted the perpetuation of regional languages) sought alliances in several European states with the Church (that feared the consequences for their religion of secular education that went along with promotion of national languages). The Church and the monopoly mediators allied to help sustain for a brief historical period an educational system that was both religious in content and regional in language. This alliance eventually collapsed given the cascade of citizens rushing to get the unmediated benefits of a national educational system and labor market.

The floral model captures the incentives for homogenization, but does not fully capture the possibility of a turning of the tides, in which regional languages regain their status as a language of authority. It is for this reason that a 'tipping' model is proposed in the next section. However, de Swaan's contribution carries with it a fundamental message, namely that ethnic entrepreneurs in peripheral regions have an immense task to convince their constituents to abjure the cultural allure of the political center. In Chapter 5, when multicultural policies are advocated, readers will be reminded that an invitation to minority groups in peripheral regions to promote their own cultures is one that young people, who have an opportunity to escape to the cosmopolitan cultural center, might well decline. Opening the gates to cultural differences will not, if the floral model has any cogency, lead to an endless flow of popularly supported claims for autonomy or secession.

Thomas Schelling's Tipping Game

An alternative way of modeling the emergence of a linguistic general will is through Nobel Prize-winning economist Thomas Schelling's tipping game, a theory of binary choice.[28] But first let us observe the intuition behind it, with an analogy from ice hockey. In the wintry ponds of Canada (or in sudden-death overtime in today's National Hockey League—NHL), ice hockey is bloody warfare, where blue lines turn to red. A culture of manliness pervaded the sport, such that wearing helmets was considered inappropriate, a signal of weakness. In my youth, no professional hockey player would wear one, and none in the NHL did. But it was possible to envision a cultural change, where wearing a helmet was normal, life-threatening injuries reduced, and reputations for manliness maintained. This would be a new culture, one not of reckless war but rather one of regulated sport. The question Schelling asked was how can cultural change happen, when the first mover to wear a helmet would be quickly humiliated and shunned? The Montreal Canadiens, the then most prestigious professional team in the NHL, whose players' manliness was never in question, provided one route to cultural change. Its goalie could don a mask at no reputation cost, and this could set off a cascade toward a new professional hockey culture. After several players followed the path set by the Canadiens' goalie, there was a certain point, in a way that Malcolm Gladwell neatly popularized,[29] at which the norm in this binary situation 'tipped' from one cultural mode to another.

Once cultural norms are shown to have tipping points, many examples of long tradition suddenly evaporating become understandable. In the early twentieth century, the long-valued Chinese tradition of footbinding rapidly disappeared. One analyst attributed this unpredicted cultural shift to a conscious strategy of parents to assure each other that each would allow their sons to marry their daughters if and only if the daughters had unbound feet. Once there was a critical mass of potential husbands for footboundless girls, Chinese culture tipped to one that valued full-footed females. In a binary choice—footbind one's daughter or not footbind—the latter quickly replaced the former as the societal norm.[30]

Application of the Tipping Game to National Identities

Consider a population with a diverse set of attributes shared through biological or cultural inheritance such as skin color, speech forms, sacred beliefs, and kinship ties.[31] People conceive of these *attributes* as qualifying them for *categorical* membership on various social *dimensions*: skin color qualifying people as members of categories such as Black and White on the dimension of race; speech forms qualifying people as members of categories such as Spanish and English on the dimension of language; sacred beliefs qualifying people as members of categories such as Christian and Muslim on the dimension of religion; and kinship ties qualifying people as members of categories such as Hawiye and Daarood on the dimension of clanship.[32]

From this perspective, the politics of ethnicity involves three major processes. People invest in attributes for purposes of qualifying for membership in another category in the process of assimilation; political entrepreneurs expand or contract category space, for example the creation of the census category 'mixed-race', to induce new coalitions; and ethnic intrepreneurs work to increase the salience of a dimension—for example, mullahs promoting religion as the salient dimension over clanship—to expand their authority.

The tipping game as applied to national identities concerns the first process; on a salient dimension—here language—people can invest to acquire a new attribute for their children, and thereby qualifying them to be members of the category of national citizens (say Spaniard). Or they can remain loyal to the language group of their region and retain membership in the category of a minority (say Catalan). The choice of a hockey helmet, therefore, has a parallel in the choice of investing in a new language, with the implication that the cumulation of such investments can substantially change the culture of a population.

To be sure—as will be elaborated in the appendix to this chapter—people can add a language to their repertoires, so language is not like wearing or not wearing a hockey helmet. They can speak both Zulu and Afrikaans.

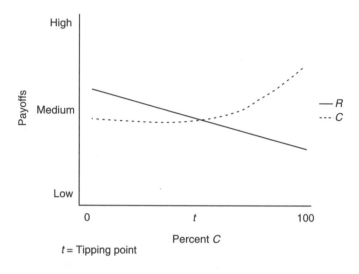

Figure 2.2. Tipping game for minorities

But the medium of instruction for primary education of children is typically a binary choice for parents. It is this choice that the model in Figure 2.2 delineates—namely the binary choice for parents to enroll their children in schools in which the medium of instruction is the language of the political center (call it *C*) or the language of their region (call it *R*). It is assumed that each parent wants her children to be educated in the common language of official business, elite discourse, and occupational mobility—that is, they want their children to speak the language of power. Parents, however, are uncertain whether their region will ultimately become a sovereign nation (in which case *R* would be the language of the new center) or whether their region will be successfully incorporated into *C*. This uncertainty induces parents to make calculations about the expected returns for their educational choices. If there are k languages that might become official, an expected utility equation of individual i would involve calculating the probability (P) of each language being chosen and her utility (U) for each language. The resulting equation is below:

$$EU_i = \sum_{\forall k} p_k U_{ik}$$

As should be evident from observation of Figure 2.2, at all points to the left of the 'tipping point' (t), a parent would benefit more (i.e. a higher payoff as recorded on the y-axis) by sending her child to schools where the medium of instruction is R. And at any point to the right of t, any parent would benefit more by sending her child to a school where C is the medium of instruction. In the world of interdependent choices, if parents see that a critical mass of other parents is moving past the tipping point in either direction, it is to the interest of all parents to participate in the cascade. In this manner, we say that the tipping game has two equilibria—meaning points on the x-axis where no parent has an incentive to change her choice—at 0% C and 100% C.[33]

This tipping model (unlike de Swaan's floral model) captures two coordination problems. On the one hand, we have a game of pure coordination. We see that 0% C (the same as 100% R) or 100% C (the same as 0% R) are each equilibria, meaning that it would be irrational (i.e. with a lower payoff) for an average individual to switch her choice. On the other hand, there is a *battle of the sexes* game as well—one where the male would prefer to have the *rendezvous* at a soccer match while the female prefers that they go to the opera, but either would prefer the choice of their partner rather than go to their preferred event alone. In the case of language choice, while some members may prefer C while others prefer R, both would prefer to coordinate rather than separate.

At each of the two equilibria—where the regional language has solidarity around a new national formation (R), or where the regional language dies and the descendants of its former speakers become part of a broader national group (C)—the outcome appears to outsiders as natural or inevitable—often called primordial and thought of as genetic—because no one has an interest in defecting from it. Yet the model shows how historically contingent the outcome was, and the product of interdependent choices. What appears obvious and inevitable *ex post* was in fact ambiguous and contingent *ex ante*. What appears as permanent is in fact reversible.

Through the lens of the tipping model, we can observe the conditions that lead to the creation of new nationalities through separation and amalgamation of cultures. With the coordination aspects of national formation modeled, my proposed definition of the nation—provided below—should be clear.

What Then Is a Nation?

Through the insights gained from the tipping model, we can now define a nation as a *population with a coordinated set of beliefs about their cultural identities* (i.e. the salient cultural dimension, their category on that dimension, and the attributes qualifying people for membership in that category) *whose representatives claim ownership of a state* (or at least an autonomous region within a state) *for them by dint of that coordination* either through separation, or amalgamation, or return.[34]

Appeals to the nation are justified by the relevant population's representatives—people I have been referring to as ethnic entrepreneurs—through the highlighting of a category on a salient dimension. These appeals are compelling to the extent that the people qualifying for membership coordinate their identities in accord with the national vision of these entrepreneurs. Nineteenth-century Zionists claimed that the category of being Jewish on the dimension of religion gave them right to ownership of Palestine; Kikuyus and Luos among other tribes in the 1950s claimed that the category of being African on the dimension of race gave them rights to own Kenya; and eastern Nigerians in the late 1960s claimed that the shared category of Igbo on the dimension of tribe gave them the right to own Biafra. The nation then is a product of cultural coordination and the claim to statehood or political autonomy for the population that successfully coordinates. Some examples follow of the coordination aspects of national formation and breakup.

STRATEGIC SEPARATION

Regional cultures, once considered slight variations on a state's national palette, can tip back into self-proclaimed nations. Reconsider Figure 2.2. Suppose the status quo is at 100% *C* reflecting full assimilation of the region into the national culture. While everyday behavior would make it seem that there is a solid national community commensurate with the boundaries of the state, there might be cultural virtuosi (consider them lonely philologists and half-forgotten poets who defied the national culture and continued to produce work in the language R most people perceived as defunct) who long for a rebirth of their ancient tongue, and a state that would embody that tongue as its national language.[35] There might as well be budding industrialists living in region R, seeking a protected market for their products from foreign competition. A new national state, in which R is the central language, might provide such a market. Political entrepreneurs emerge and work to ally cultural virtuosi with the budding entrepreneurs into a common nationalist movement. These entrepreneurs, to fulfill their program, will try to revive defunct national cultures, and move their communities from 100% C toward the tipping point t, en route to their utopia of 100% R.

Catalans in Spain

Catalonia, a region of northeastern Spain and southwestern France, has long had all the 'objective' conditions for a modern nation-state. By the thirteenth century, its kingdom under Jaume I (the Conqueror) controlled a not inconsiderable territory, had its own representative institutions, and ruled over a society with a thriving literature in the national language—Catalan. Yet with the reconquest of the Iberian Peninsula by the Catholic Monarchs (Ferdinand and Isabela) in the fifteenth century, throughout the period of Habsburg rule, and culminating with the victory of the Bourbons in the War of Spanish Succession (that ended in the early eighteenth century), Catalonia was slowly but inexorably incorporated into the Spanish state. The very first books printed on the peninsula using the Gutenberg Press were in Catalan; but by the end of the seventeenth century, virtually all books printed in Catalonia were in Castilian. Although Catalan remained the mother tongue of most Catalans (thereby making Castilian only *quasi*-hegemonic), all Catalans recognized that Castilian had to be a key component of their language repertoires, and the language of higher learning and official business. We can say that the Catalan region in the late seventeenth century was moving toward the 100% C equilibrium in the tipping game.[36]

In response to the cascade to Castilian (increasingly called 'Spanish'), national revival movements dominated Catalan politics in three distinct periods in the modern era. In the late nineteenth century, the Catalan lonely philologists and half-forgotten poets were glorified by a new industrial bourgeoisie seeking protection for their goods from English imports. Central authorities refused to comply, and these industrialists petitioned for an economic separation from Madrid by demanding their own national state, justified by the need to sustain the ancient Catalan culture. During a brief moment of democracy in the period from 1931 to 1936, Catalans voted for and received autonomy from the Spanish center, in the hope of promoting their national language and protecting their local industrialists. Their initial success was a major reason why General Francisco Franco toppled the democratic regime with the goal of preserving a unitary Spain. After his military victory (in a three-year civil war), Franco brutally suppressed the Catalan revival movement for a generation. With the dictator's death and the rise of a modern democracy, the Catalan revival reemerged, and this time succeeded in making Catalan the principal language of education and administration (in a campaign called 'linguistic normalization'), even if (in the context of the Spanish state) all Catalans were expected to maintain across generations full fluency in Spanish. Completing the tip, nearly all schoolchildren in today's Catalan autonomous region of Spain are taught *in* Catalan.

If 100% *C* were an equilibrium, how did the advocates of 'linguistic normalization' succeed? After all, if every Spaniard spoke Spanish and Spanish is spoken widely in many countries of the world, an education in Catalan gains children no life advantages. Indeed, many Catalans who voted for normalization subverted it by sending their children abroad for education or to French- or English-dominant foreign schools in Catalonia. Yet the linguistic normalization movement largely succeeded in creating coordinated expectations among fellow Catalans that the region would tip in the direction of a 100% *R* equilibrium.

To foster that tip, and recognizing the hurdles of an equilibrium shift, Catalan nationalists employed a variety of tactics. First, the Catalan autonomous government made side payments to authors who published their works in Catalan. The government knew that since the payoff for using Spanish was *on average* higher for any writer (given the enormous relative size of the Spanish-reading public internationally), a side payment to an individual was necessary to make *her* payoff higher for using Catalan. Thus the government committed itself to the purchase of a sufficient number of exemplars of any book published in Catalan to assure the author and the press a profit. Catalan state TV was also heavily subsidized, and the hottest American soap operas were dubbed into Catalan at the regional government's expense in order to raise the average benefit to individuals for learning Catalan.

The move toward *t* was still not assured. In response to the slow progress of Catalanization, several vigilante groups emerged. Among them were *Crida a la Solidaridat* ('Appeal to Solidarity') and *Terra Lliure* ('Free Land'). They took it upon themselves to deface signs written in Castilian and to humiliate state officials who used Castilian. Humiliation raised the costs for Catalans when they used Spanish in public. Slowly, as the public came to believe that the movement toward *t* was inevitable, they 'voted' (in that metaphoric plebiscite) for *R* in fear of being in the future minority. The point here is that regional revivals do not succeed only with a majority sentiment in their favor; they require for success the expectation of all individuals that all other individuals expect the revival to succeed and have conditioned their behavior (most importantly, in where to send children to school) on that expectation.

COMPETITIVE ASSIMILATION

Let us now examine examples of a reverse cascade— one toward full acceptance by immigrant minorities of a national language different from their own mother tongues. In this game, the starting equilibrium is at 0% *C* for the immigrant population, as they all speak the language of their homeland. They have to decide whether to support medium of instruction education in their home language so that their children will remain loyal to their homeland culture or to enroll them in schools where the dominant language of their new country is the medium of instruction and to hasten their assimilation into the culture of their adopted homeland.

Castilian-Speakers in Catalonia

A substantial minority of immigrants (from poorer regions of Spain such as Andalucía, all of them Spanish-speakers) were induced to move to Catalonia during the Franco period, in part to serve as a workforce for industrial development, but also in part to de-Catalanize Catalonia. With some one-third of the population non-Catalans, Franquist bureaucrats reasoned, how could Catalonia possibly become an autonomous national government? Catalan language entrepreneurs had a deep strategic problem in getting these immigrants to vote themselves (which they would do only if they expected other immigrants to do so) as Catalans. In order to get Spanish-speaking immigrants to learn the dominant regional language, Catalans had to convince migrants that the Catalanist project would succeed. One tactic was to make credible their threat that all future job openings in Catalonia would require facility in Catalan. They did this through a solidarity pact among businessmen that the language of all big business would be conducted in Catalan. Seeing this, immigrant families feared that if their children did not speak Catalan, they would not be accepted into university, would not be competitive for civil service jobs, and would not easily move into Catalonia's middle class. Immigrant families recognized a further logic—namely, that if their children learned Catalan faster than their neighbors' children, their children would have an advantage in the labor market. Each immigrant family sought to Catalanize first! This is the strategic logic of 'competitive assimilation'.

Russian-Speaking Populations in the Near-Abroad

After the breakup of the Soviet Union, the nationalizing elites of Estonia faced a similar problem as the language entrepreneurs of Catalonia. During the post-World War II period, after it incorporated Estonia, the Soviet regime induced more than a half-million Russian-speakers (mostly Russians, but also Ukrainians, Belarusans, and Jews) to settle in northeastern Estonia to rebuild the bombed areas and to man factories and defense establishments. By the time Estonia broke from the Union in 1991, one-third of its population had no Estonian cultural roots and hardly any facility in the Estonian language. The Estonian nationalizing elite recognized that it could not repatriate these Russian-speakers, as many were born in Estonia and had no home to which they could return. But also, forced repatriation was anathema to Europeans, and the Estonian elite did not want to risk future membership in the EU by showing an illiberal face.

The alternative, if there was to be an Estonian nation-state with a single dominant culture, was to induce the

Russian-speakers to adopt Estonian cultural practices, most notably the language. That is to say, the Estonian goal was to move the Russian-speaking population from an equilibrium of 100% R (where R is Russian, the language of the old center but the new region) to a new equilibrium where all Estonian citizens relied principally on Estonian for public affairs at 100% C. Estonian political and cultural leaders sought to do this by changing the benefits and costs for Russian-speakers who had to rethink the value of the language repertoires appropriate for their children. The nationalizing government raised the costs for maintaining Russian monolingualism by denying citizenship to any Russian who could not pass an examination in Estonian. More coercively, in an implicit solidarity pact, Estonians refused to maintain Russian in their children's repertoires. This became a credible threat to Russian-speakers that if their children did not learn Estonian, future communications with political authority would require translation services.

Not only did the Estonian government raise the costs for Russians to maintain monolingual repertoires, but it also raised the benefits to them for speaking Estonian by making certain jobs available only to Estonian-speakers. These acts set off a competitive assimilation dynamic, as young Russian-speakers realized the advantages that would accrue to them should they learn Estonian better than their peers. Soon there were waiting lists for the few Estonian-medium schools in the northeast of the country. And summer programs that brought Russian-speakers to Estonian rural areas for acculturation were quickly oversubscribed.[37] Once Russian-speakers saw an inevitability of the 100% C

equilibrium, many of them wanted their children to be there first! This initiated moves that could lead to a full cascade. Though in the real world the road is bumpier than the formal model shows, and the time it will take for the cascade to occur is in generations and not years, there is a discernible trend toward a unified nation-state of Estonians, composed of some one-third of the population that will trace its ancestry to Russian-speakers.

STRATEGIC STASIS

Those who portray nationalism as the culmination of a natural alliance between race, culture, and the state cannot easily account for Andalucianos becoming Catalans or Russian-speakers becoming Estonians. But a rational choice model based on utility maximization, as with the tipping game, faces its own anomalies. How to account for the continued existence of despised marginal groups in a society, whose members would apparently have all incentives to assimilate and thereby enjoy the life chances of the dominant group in society? Groups such as Jews in early modern Europe, Harijans (or Untouchables) in India, and Roma (Gypsies) throughout modern Europe are examples of despised groups that persist. Can the tipping model give insight as to why there is stasis when it would appear rational for each marginal person to vote himself or herself out of his or her ascribed identity? And if each made the same rational decision, would not the entire group disappear from the historical stage?[38]

Marginals, indeed, are like any minority population whose members reckon the payoffs for assimilation and

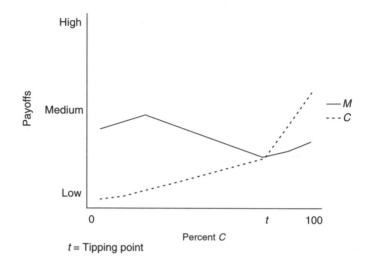

Figure 2.3. Tipping game for marginals

compare them to those of cultural retention. However, groups whose payoffs for assimilating are very low at the early stages of assimilation opportunities—a defining characteristic of marginals—are not likely ever to take a risk and move toward assimilation. An analysis of Figure 2.3 shows the consequences for assimilation when groups face lower payoffs for early assimilation.

Compare Figure 2.3's tipping game for marginals with Figure 2.2, the tipping game for regional minority groups. It has the same structure as Figure 2.2, but with two important differences. First, even though the payoffs for individuals at 0% C (or 100% M, M referring to the payoff for marginals) are far lower than that of assimilation at 100% C (making assimilation better for the average marginal than maintenance of marginal status), the gap in payoffs at 0% C between assimilation and the status quo (in favor of the status quo) is much greater for the average marginal than the regional minority. This implies a heavy cost for any 'first mover' into the assimilationist camp. Why should this be so? Jews, the Harijans, and the Roma were all consigned to economic roles that were more lucrative (banking for Jews, cleaning of streets and other essential tasks for Harijans, and seasonal labor for Roma) than the jobs at the bottom rung of the regular labor market. Therefore, the payoff for a marginal if he retained monopoly rights to the despised economic role was higher than if he sought to integrate into the dominant cultural group. Given this reserved and despised economic role, the payoff for assimilation, if it were to yield higher returns, would require extensive retraining. Therefore, an investment in assimilation for returns on wages would hardly be positive, especially for the first movers.

Second, the tipping point 't' is much later in the game for marginals than minority groups in general. This means that a higher percentage of them must assimilate before it is rational for the next unassimilated marginal to assimilate. This is so for two reasons. The first reason has to do with social acceptance for assimilation by members of the dominant culture. The more identifiable marginals are from the dominant cultural groups in society—what Gellner has called 'entropy resistant' characteristics[39]—the easier it is for the dominant group to police attempts by marginals from entering their social world. If the costs of assimilating are high, and the benefits restricted even as many marginals attempt to 'pass', we should expect those who try to pass to suffer humiliations as they apply for membership to clubs and enter the marriage market associated with the dominant group. The humiliation suffered by the would-be passers would lower the benefits of assimilation and thereby push the tipping point to the right.

Internal dynamics are equally at work. Marginal communities are commonly isolated socially and spatially from the dominant group. Within these marginal communities, elites develop status and influence that they would lose should their constituents leave the community for membership in the wider society. Among the Jews in Eastern Europe, rabbis were conservative antiassimilationist elites. In nineteenth century Hungary, rabbis joined forces to prevent the reading of sermons in the languages of the nations. To be sure, other Jewish elites, such as the merchants, had conflicting interests in favor of assimilation. But the rabbis, given the nature of the ghettos in which Jews lived, had considerable cultural influence in policing potential assimilators. They also had an interest in such policing, as their social influence would decrease as assimilation increased.

Not only elites police. Norms of solidarity form as well among nonelites in marginal populations, as they all face common oppression. Among Harijans, for example, the poorest of the poor enforce norms of separation by revealing the identities of comrades who tried to 'pass' as caste Hindus. Under these conditions, early assimilators are threats both to the future leadership of elites and to the community norms of nonelites. Punishment of assimilators as 'sellouts' will consequently be more intense, and it will take a greater mass of assimilators to override collective antiassimilationist policing.

Thus despite the fact that the 'will of all' among marginals might be to become part of the dominant culture, given a theory of interdependent choice, it would be irrational for any one of them to 'vote' for assimilation—going back to Renan's metaphor—as an individual on this matter. None could be sure, given that many fellow marginals would not assimilate, that there would ever be an assimilationist cascade. Thus it was rational for each to remain at 0% C. To be sure, over the centuries many Jews, Harijans, and Roma 'passed' as members of the dominant cultural groups in the countries in which they lived. But a critical mass of each of these groups has both suffered and persisted over the centuries.

THE THREE FACTORS THAT GO INTO 'TIPS'

The principal mechanism influencing individual decisions to retain or change their linguistic repertoires is the position on the x-axis, that is, on how many other people in their community have changed or are likely to change their linguistic repertoire. This is what makes the choices by individuals interdependent—each is looking to how others will choose. But three other factors influence the relative size of the payoffs for each choice at each point on the x-axis.[40]

Economic Payoffs

As with de Swaan's 'floral model', parents calculate the job prospects for the language repertoires of their children. In the Catalan normalization project, an important aspect of the choice of Andalucian-heritage parents was the hope that their children would not inherit their parents' blue-collar jobs, but rather join the middle class as policemen, store clerks, and local government administrators. All of these upwardly mobile jobs would require, in their reckoning, facility in Catalan. This is to say, independent of the number of Andalucian parents who chose the Catalan language as the medium of instruction for their children, the economic payoff for doing so was alluring. In the case of the Harijans, and especially the sweepers, the economic payoff from marginality was for a long time higher than returns from joining the caste economy. This lowered the incentive to invest in passing as a caste Hindu.

This economic motive is quite important in analyzing nationality choice. Through much of India, parents hedge their linguistic bets in order to maximize their expected yield for their linguistic investments. It is common for families (especially in trade) to provide English education for one child, French for another, and German for a third. All possible transactions are covered![41] In Ghana, parents are happy to give up a latent desire to promote a national language in order to optimize for their children the opportunities for exploiting the international job market that operates in English. English as the medium of instruction in Ghanaian schools is preferred not because it represents national unity, but rather because it opens economic opportunity.[42]

But economic motives are not always decisive. After all, the Catalans had no expectations for economic gain by the promotion of the Catalan language in the school system.

In the new states carved from the former Soviet Union, economic payoffs were similarly discounted. The Russian diaspora in the breakaway states had to decide whether to have their children educated in the new national languages of their 'titular' republics. Parents were more influenced by the status gains and losses involved in switching than they were by economic gains. It is to those status issues that I now turn.

In-Group Status

A second component of the payoff function concerns levels of social support and stigma given by members of a community for the identity choices made by their peers. Stigma is often attached by peers to those who assimilate. In the USA, for example, many African-Americans have opprobrium heaped upon them by other African-Americans should they be seen dating someone from the White community, or if they are heard 'speaking White' or impressing White teachers with extra credit homework assignments completed. During a regional separation dynamic, the stigma is attached to those whose ancestors are of the regional culture but who themselves identify with the state culture in which they were brought up and educated.

Social stigma requires a form of in-group policing, in which members of the group threatened by movement across the x-axis toward 100% C mobilize fellow members of the community to humiliate and even threaten assimilators, who are treated as cultural traitors. Policing is organized by those who feel they can be the spokespersons for a newly emerging nationality, but would lose their power should their group 'disappear' through assimilation. During the height of the Basque regional revival, for example, families that sent their children to Spanish-language schools were harassed by Basque nationalists. Harassment certainly raised the costs of assimilation by people of Basque heritage into the Spanish state.

In-group status has its positive, or social support side, as well. If the economic returns for speaking English, the language of Europe, are high, parents in Norway, as is modeled in Chapter 4, may still want to enroll their children in state—that is Norwegian medium—schools. One reason is that to study Norwegian literature and to participate in the jokes and intrigues of schoolyard dramas, children are building up a form of cultural capital that will allow them to function effortlessly in Norwegian society. There are status rewards in being able to understand the puns and allusions of one's own culture, as they provide what Hardin has called 'the epistemological comforts of home'.[43]

Out-Group Acceptance

Out-group acceptance is the other side of the coin from in-group status. There is out-group acceptance when members of the assimilating community receive status within the majority community that rewards them for adapting to new cultural practices.[44] During Third Republic France, Bretons, Catalans, Alsatians, and Provençals could migrate to Paris, and if they learned the French language and the mores of cuisine and dress, they could join French society commensurate with their social class. Out-group acceptance hastened assimilation.

But out-group rejection yields lower rates of assimilation. Suppose a member of R (call her r), or a member of M (call her m), learns the language C, and gets a job commensurate with her skills. Suppose as well, as was alluded to in the discussion of marginals, that she is shunned from C society, not invited to its clubs, and denied access to its marriage market. This was certainly the case among black Africans in South Africa during the period of National Party rule. It is largely the case for Arab citizens in Israel, even before the first Intifada. For the Jews in Weimar Germany, the situation of out-group acceptance was a bit more ironic. The Jews assiduously studied high German culture, its opera, theater, and literature. But the Germans abandoned these arenas, and when Jews attended German opera, they joined the society only of other Jews.[45] While Jews tried hard to assimilate, they could not erase their social stigma, with disastrous consequences after Weimar's fall. To the extent that the payoff for assimilating activities leads to little out-group acceptance, future rs or ms will adjust their estimations of the payoffs for assimilation downward, and thereby slow any movement toward t, the tip to assimilation.

CONCLUSION

Ernest Renan was correct to point out in 1882 that nations are the products neither of nature nor of descent, but rather of choice. Renan's telling examples and the vignettes herein of Catalans in Spain, Andalucianos in Catalonia, and Russian-speakers in Estonia demonstrate the historical contingency of national identifications, and the possibility of intergenerational shift.

Yet Renan's metaphor of a daily plebiscite was misleading, or a half-truth. People do not vote for their nationality as they do for a set of political alternatives because the principal goal in this sort of election is not to win, but to choose the national identity that most others in one's community are likely to choose. When it comes to national identities, we are not in competition with our neighbors but rather in coordination with them. Coordination among large numbers of people, however, is not easy to accomplish, even if all the people agree on a preferred outcome. Thus the role of ethnic entrepreneurs.

It is the social reality of interdependent choice and the desire for coordination that makes nations seem natural—since they represent votes that are very difficult to reverse. But at certain historical moments change can be rapid, as in a cascade. The tipping model illustrates both the sense of permanence *and* the fragility of national identifications. More important, it illustrates that the primordial image of society, where class is dynamic due to opportunities for social mobility while nationality is static without any expectations of cultural mobility, is flawed.

APPENDIX

Why Language?

If the salient dimension for national membership can be race, religion, or language, it is natural to wonder why the focus of this book is so intent on language. Of course, this is only a partial truth.[46] Indeed, each of these other dimensions can be separately analyzed through the tipping model as described in this chapter, and each would give a somewhat different slant to the progress of assimilation or differentiation in any society. Emphasizing one dimension, language, as I do here, gives only a partial view of national evolutions, but it allows for a more concrete and sustained discussion of the tipping phenomenon, and this is why it is highlighted in this book.

It should be acknowledged, however, that language has special attributes that make it especially amenable to the vision of the nation that is promoted herein. Unlike monotheistic religion and race, language is not exclusive, and potential assimilants can learn a new language adding to their cultural repertoires without giving up their ancestral tongues, or really changing their cultural beliefs or identities. Yet unlike dress or music, choices about acquiring language are not subject to fashions and fads—learning a language has heavy opportunity costs. Therefore, unlike race, changes in language repertoires are possible within a generation. And unlike religion, changes in language can be additive and need not imply any change in belief or deep-seated identity. People may learn the language merely to get a taxi license, neither more nor less. The assumption here is that people may learn a language for purely instrumental reasons. Meanwhile the intergenerational consequences of language shift have powerful implications for identity. But that is an assumption. And finally, unlike dress and music, changes in language cannot be done on a whim. Language shift therefore is both possible and costly. This is the image of assimilation that is neatly portrayed in the Schelling model, and the cogency of the model is in large part a result of the cultural dimension used to exemplify it. There is thus a danger (generalizing from a unique cultural dimension) and a beauty (using a cultural dimension that tracks identity in a clear manner) in using language shift as a measure for cultural assimilation or separation.

CHAPTER 3

The Cultural Foundations of Nationalism

'The language relativity theory [holds] that users of markedly different grammars are pointed by their grammars toward different types of observation and different evaluations of externally similar acts of observation, and hence are not equivalent as observers but must arrive at somewhat different view of the world.'

Benjamin Lee Whorf in *Language, Thought and Reality*

IF nations are merely the result of coordination dynamics, as was implied in Chapter 2, do they lack any cultural content? Is the coordination on national membership like coordinating on which side of the road to drive on, or whether it is best to pronounce 'controversy' with its accent on the first or second syllable? In this chapter, to answer these questions, a Janus-faced approach to the study of culture is introduced. From one perspective, and consistent with the coordination approach to nationality, an equilibrium notion of culture is proposed.[47] Here culture is seen as a resource enabling collective action. Yet from a second perspective, another research tradition shows how the transmission of culture sustains distinct norms, beliefs, and even—as asserted by Whorf in the epigraph to this chapter—worldviews. Reconciling these two faces of culture is essential for any understanding of how cultures (and nations) coordinate and what they coordinate on.

AN EQUILIBRIUM APPROACH TO CULTURE

In the movie 'The Matrix'—today's version of the Platonic cave—ordinary people are caught in a web of meaning and control that is so pervasive that they do not even know that they are engulfed. Anthropologists are fond of metaphors like webs and matrices to describe the impact of culture on individuals.[48] The definition of culture offered here seeks, against this metaphoric consensus in Cultural Anthropology, to delimit the range of culture while at the same time highlighting its social, economic, and political impact.

Before a definition of culture is proposed—and it will be a mouthful—consider this Somali example.[49] Maxamad Siyaad Barre led a military *coup d'état* to capture state power in Somalia in 1969 and quickly allied with his Soviet patrons to declare the Democratic Republic of Somalia that was to be built on the principles of scientific socialism.[50] Riding a wave of popular support from virtually all Somali clans, in 1977 he took advantage of revolutionary anarchy in Ethiopia and arms supplied to him by his Soviet patrons in order to incorporate through military conquest the Ogaadeen, a largely Somali-populated desert region of Ethiopia on the western border of Somalia. The Soviets were nonplussed by this unexpected move, and besides, preferred to ally with the newly self-proclaimed Marxist regime in Ethiopia, a country far richer and more influential than Somalia could ever be. Soviet advisers crossed the Ogaadeen in support of their new clients and then helped decimate the near-victorious Somali army. In retreat in 1978, the Somali army and society broke apart in self-recrimination and clan rivalry.

Defeated in war, President Siyaad faced imminent rebellion by leaders from disfavored clans, whom he brutally suppressed. But to further protect himself, as the war against him became threatening by 1980, he appointed a heralded general from the Ogaadeen war, Maxamad Caali Samantar, as both his Prime Minister and Minister of Defense. Samantar came from an outcaste Somali group whom among other restrictions no 'clan' Somali father would allow his daughter to marry. His role, from the President's strategic vision, was to run interference for the President against his opposition. Siyaad's was a brilliant move. The idea that such a man could serve as president was anathema both to those clans supporting and to those seeking to overthrow the president. It was common knowledge that Samantar, if he led a coup, would get no public support. Therefore, all officers knew that coup-talk in the barracks by any officers would be considered by all other Somali officers as fantastic and unimaginable. Because all officers knew that all other officers shared Somali cultural beliefs, they knew a coup that respected army rank would fail to get popular support. And Siyaad, who knew what his officer corps knew—and knew that they knew that he knew it—was in the relatively easy position of having to protect the life of his Minister of Defense as a first line of defense in protection of his own incumbency. Siyaad's rule, taking advantage of Somali cultural beliefs, persisted for another eleven years.

However much they were deterred, it would be incorrect to say that Somali officers were imprisoned in a cultural matrix. Dealing with outcastes was a small part of their lives, and they were perfectly willing to take orders from then-Brigadier-General Samantar, a logistical genius, when the army was marching on to Jigjiga, a major Somali-populated city of the Ogaadeen. Yet because of common knowledge about a taboo, their freedom of action in devising a coup was seriously restricted. They would not move first because they knew that their fellow officers and the general population would not follow.

With this example in mind, consider an alternative definition to that proposing culture as a matrix. In its stead, let us define *culture* as an *equilibrium in a well-defined set of circumstances in which members of a group sharing in common descent, symbolic practices and/or high levels of interaction*—and thereby becoming a cultural group—*are able to condition their behavior on common knowledge beliefs about the behavior of all members of the group.*[51]

This definition requires some unpacking. A cultural group is a delimited set of people who because of common descent or high levels of interaction can readily identify one another as members of a group and determine who are nonmembers. Members of a cultural group typically share a set of symbolic practices such as language, religion, artistic forms, and rituals (marking births, marriages, and deaths). By these criteria, the Somalis are a cultural group.

Common knowledge is a cognitive criterion that is met when all members of a group have knowledge about a set of things, know as well that all members of the group have this knowledge, know as well that all members of the group know that all others have this knowledge, and so on.[52] Through shared symbols and high levels of interaction, cultural groups such as the Somalis develop cultural beliefs (e.g. about who is an outcaste) that meet the condition of common knowledge. In interactions with other members of their cultural group, cultural group members condition their behavior on this common knowledge, as did the President and Samantar's fellow officers.

Cultural beliefs are common knowledge beliefs shared by members of a cultural group about what a member of the group would do under a range of conditions (such as whether to support a General, who happened to be an outcaste, in an otherwise much-wanted coup), including many circumstances, as will be elaborated on below, that are rarely if ever observed. Therefore, cultural beliefs are outside any individual's control (we say, 'exogenous' to any individual) but an essential feature in understanding group behavior (we say, 'endogenous' to the group in which he or she is a member).[53]

A circumstance is a well-defined sequence of interactions among members of the group, as would be the case in the execution of a *coup d'état*, since it has a well-understood sequence of moves possibly leading to coordination among members of an officer corps. In Chapter 2, the moment of school choice the parents face for their children represents a circumstance.

A cultural equilibrium exists when members of a cultural group have overriding incentives in a range of circumstances to behave in the manner prescribed by their culture. Taking others' behavior as given, each individual's incentive in a particular circumstance covered by her culture is to behave in a manner prescribed by that culture. In the case of President Siyaad, the path of play leading to 'no coup attempt' along with 'careful presidential attention to the safety of his Minister of Defense and his ability to maintain control over the military hierarchy' constitutes an equilibrium.

The notion of an equilibrium suggests that there is a rationally founded path of play based on each actor's best reply to any move that other actors may make. One implication of a game theoretic approach is that common knowledge also includes beliefs about what members of a cultural group are likely to do under a range of circumstances not yet envisioned. And thus, when members of a cultural group encounter unexpected behaviors from other members that are 'off the equilibrium path', that is, behaviors that would never occur if all members of the group were to have engaged in 'backwards induction' to compute the optimum path of play, they would need to respond with improvised action, perhaps to devise sanctions, but in accord with common knowledge of what other members of the group would do in similar circumstances.[54] An outcaste leading a coup is off the path of play (and in fact no such coup has ever taken place in Somalia), but due to common knowledge, all officers could infer their optimal response should such a circumstance have arisen.

To summarize the Somali example, the equilibrium approach to culture helps interpret the success of President Siyaad's tactic for limiting the risk of a coup. Samantar's performance in the then recent military campaigns made him a plausible choice as Vice-President and Minister of Defense. Yet being from an outcaste group meant that few could imagine him as president. He knew that planning a coup would be useless since his outcaste status implied that he would receive insufficient political support to remain as president even if he and a junta behind him occupied and claimed control over the presidential palace. This, in turn, gave him the incentive to carefully police the military to prevent coups from more junior officers. This behavior is part of an equilibrium in the sense that it is supported by a combination of self-interest and cultural beliefs. Samantar's interests were allied with the President's because he knew he could never himself be president. Although he could have attempted a coup, he knew that such an act would not succeed in making him president for any extended period. He thus refrained from it.

Contra the anthropological tradition that sees culture as ubiquitous and indivisible, equilibrium theory suggests that culture can be subject to analysis, that is to say, broken down into its component parts. Once done, cultural analysis can provide clear and simple answers to big questions. Why, for example, do individuals follow the behavioral expectations inherent in culture? The equilibrium answer is that they must have incentives to do so. Why, to ask a related question, are individuals so heavily influenced by cultural norms? The equilibrium answer is that through common knowledge they expect other members of their culture to act that way and to police those norms.

DO CULTURES EMBED BELIEFS?

But cultural beliefs go beyond coordination; they include beliefs about what members share in common as members of a cultural group. Mormons value polygyny. French value food. Balinese value theater. And Americans value work. But it is not obvious what to make of these claims. Are these cultural inheritances, like green eyes or susceptibility to Crohn's syndrome?[55] And, if so, where is the DNA assuring faithful transmission? Perhaps they are tastes that are inculcated in youth over the generations that sustain traditional practices? But if they are merely tastes, why do they not change like the length of women's skirts? Social scientists have long sought answers to questions of cultural transmission, but few propositions on these matters have withstood critical scrutiny. Partly for this reason, accounting for differences in culture and then specifying the implications of cultural difference for social, economic, and political behavior is a project that has been largely abandoned by anthropologists today.

But at the turn of the twentieth century, there was promising research in the social sciences that linked culture to social and economic behavior. In 1905, the German sociologist Max Weber published an essay that was a breakthrough in linking culture to behavior.[56] He noticed that Protestant Europe was rich while Catholic Europe was comparatively poor. He attributed the capitalist success of Protestants to an 'ethic' that emerged from the Calvinist doctrine of predestination. This doctrine held that only the elect would attain salvation. While mortals could never know whether they were chosen by God, they would get positive assurances if they lived an ascetic yet hard-working life. Going to work at a precisely specified morning hour, working all day, earning money without spending it, all these were signs of election. For Calvin's Swiss adherents, it was natural to think that it was godly for personal lives to run like clocks. The resulting patterns of behavior, in which money was reinvested rather than used for consumption, where double-entry bookkeeping was seen as God's work, and where promptness was considered a godly virtue, had an elective affinity with the 'spirit of capitalism'. Here culture (religious beliefs) drove economic behavior (modern capitalism).

In this same period, Franz Boas and colleagues, like Weber, advocated a cultural approach to understanding human behavior. Weberians focused on religion in a fight against the economic materialists; Boasians (the founders of the Anthropology Department of Columbia University) focused on nature in a fight against the biological reductionists who saw the foundations of human behavior in nature. Two of Boas's leading acolytes were Margaret Mead and Ruth Benedict, both of whom related cultural practices in childrearing to subsequent behavior by adolescents and soldiers. Mead argued *inter alia* that cultural practices of bodily exposure of adults to children in Samoa reduced the emotional problems in adolescence that poisoned relations between mothers and their daughters in the USA.

Benedict highlighted the surrender to death ratio among Japanese troops in World War II as the lowest in modern warfare. She explained the refusal to surrender by a focus on the culture of shame in Japanese childrearing.[57]

Perhaps the most ingenious (quasi-)Boasian (though influenced by Edward Sapir, also teaching anthropology at Columbia) was an insurance inspector named Benjamin Lee Whorf, quoted at the beginning of this chapter. In his work, he recognized the crucial impact that language had on behavior. For example, he observed workers smoking next to what they called 'empty gasoline cans'. Indeed, they were empty of liquid gasoline. But allowing workers to smoke next to gas fumes was a fire hazard. Our use of the word 'empty' to refer to solids and liquids but not gases was a source of dangerous behavior that workers did not even consider as risky. Whorf's linguistic epiphany led him to Columbia University to study with Sapir and then to devote his life to research on the Hopi living in the American southwest—where he could gain insight by comparing a truly foreign language with what Whorf later referred to as Standard Average European—with brilliant insights on such things as the lack of Hopi tenses and the resultant everyday focus on duration of events rather than their onset.[58]

These studies linking culture to behavior all suffered from a near fatal flaw, namely that their authors could not demonstrate that the causal arrow went in the direction from culture to behavior. For example, Weber never considered the reverse hypothesis—namely that Europeans who had within them a 'spirit of capitalism' needed to break away from the grip of the Vatican, its tithes and suspicion of all entrepreneurial behavior. Protestantism from this viewpoint was the result of a spirit of capitalism rather than its cause.[59]

Influenced by the Weberian/Boasian research traditions, and by the excitement of African independence in the 1960s, I inquired whether there would be a return to African culture once the colonial powers were in retreat. Despite calls for 'négritude' and 'African personality' that pervaded the ideology of African nationalism, most African countries retained French and English as their languages of formal education and state administration. Serving as an American Peace Corps Volunteer in Somalia, I asked: Does it make an observable difference in behavior if all Somalis speak to each other (or educate their children, or write official memos) in Somali, as opposed to the colonial languages of English, French, Italian, or Amharic, or the language of their religious instruction (Arabic)?

To answer this question, and partially to address the fatal flaw of reverse causation, I set up a field experiment in the Somali town of Wajir, in Kenya's northeastern province.[60] Enlisting secondary students who were bilingual in Somali and English as subjects, I conducted role-playing sessions. In the first of them, I assigned one student the role of headmaster of a secondary school and his or her partner the role of teacher. Student respondents were told that the teacher had set a practice test for the students before taking their external examinations. The headmaster saw the examination and summoned the teacher to his or her office, demanding that the teacher revise the examination, for as it stood it was, in the headmaster's judgment, too easy. The student who played the headmaster was assigned the task of initiating the conversation, ordering the teacher to revise the examination he or she set.

In the sixteen dialogues that played themselves out on this theme (half in English, half in Somali, with the students being told at the start of the session which language they would be using), there were two typical tropes. First was the issue of which examination would best prepare the students for the external evaluation. This trope I considered to be 'pedagogical' in the sense that the two role players argued over issues of what would provide students with the best chance at succeeding at the subsequent and more important level. The second trope turned on who had the right to set the examination, the headmaster or the teacher. This trope I considered to be based on 'authority', that is, who was the rightful decider.

My hypothesis was that because Somali culture was highly egalitarian without clearly demarked authority roles, and because its language did not allow for easy claims based on authority, the Somali-language dialogues would be more likely to turn on pedagogy. Meanwhile, phrases such as 'I am the headmaster and the rules of the Ministry of Education give me the right to determine educational policies in this school' are common in English. In consequence, hypothesized, the English-language dialogues would be more likely to turn on authority.

Figures 3.1 and 3.2 present the results.[61] Pedagogical claims (ones based on substantive criteria) were more often used in the Somali-language dialogues; authority claims (ones based on roles and the authority granted to people who had those roles) were more common in the English-language dialogues. Here the exogenous selection of the

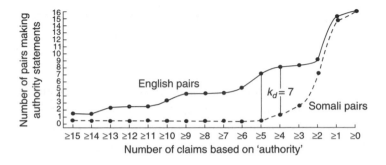

Figure 3.1. Somali and English dialogues on authority claims

language for interaction—with language seen as an element of culture—drove behavior. The choice of a national language, it can be inferred, was much more than a choice of which side of the road to drive on. Through everyday linguistic practices, it embedded common knowledge beliefs about appropriate criteria for resolving conflicts.

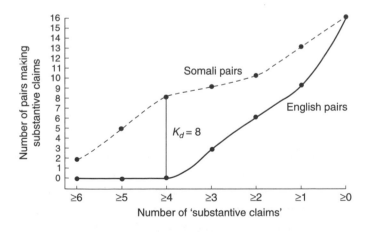

Figure 3.2. Somali and English dialogues on substantive claims

Beliefs about the criteria for conflict resolution, induced by cultural framing, reveal culture's second face.

That people share a culture that structures their political behavior, it should be emphasized, does not imply that they all share the same values, as often attributed to culture by those who see it as a matrix. It defies everyday observation to imagine that Israelis, or Japanese, or Chileans— even if we could say they each shared a common culture—share values. Rather, they share what Metzger has called—in reference to neo-Confucian China—'points of concern'. By this he means issues that members of the cultural group feel are important enough to argue about. Israelis, for example, disagree deeply as to the boundaries of the Jewish homeland, but they cannot trivialize its importance as a shared point of concern. It is shared (or common knowledge) beliefs about these points of concern that distinguish cultural groups as groups.[62]

THE SALIENCE OF CULTURE

In a subsequent research project conducted in the late 1970s, I asked whether religion (as in Weber's thesis) could have the same effect as language.[63] I conducted field research in southwestern Nigeria where the Yoruba people had been exposed to both Christianity and Islam at the same point in their history, for about the same reasons— as potential adherents aligned themselves with power and trade. Since there was no difference (as reported by historians) in who among the Yoruba became Christian and Muslim at the time of conversion, experiments that found differences between these two religious subsets of Yorubas (among the grandchildren of the original converts) could attribute those differences to the religious experience itself rather than a third variable such as the factors that went into the original conversion.

Muslims and Christians were expected to diverge on several factors. For example, Anglican Christians were expected to find authority in the scriptures, and to define a good life from the morals, the admonitions, and the exemplary behavior of the savior. Meanwhile, the Sunni Muslims were expected to find authority in the interpretations of their imam, whoever he might be, coming from his Friday sermons.[64] Indeed, authority in the church and the mosque that I attended weekly over the course of a year was exerted in a manner reflecting these two different religious cultures. However, in a series of interviews with adherents from both religious communities, there were no differences whatsoever in how they reacted to political authority in the context of Nigerian politics.

Instead, the relevant cultural dimension separating Yorubas was not religion, but their 'ancestral city' (called subtribe in Nigerian discourse), that is, the Yoruba city of their ancestors, no matter where they were living in the late 1970s. And so, Yorubas politicked with intensity for intercity advantage. In response to the first face of culture (the cultural equilibrium face), Yorubas used their sharing of tribal identification to foster coordination and political gain among those from the same ancestral city background. Meanwhile Yorubas sought no political advantage in playing the religious card, even though Yoruba Muslims could have allied with Muslim Northerners (non-Yorubas) to great economic, political, and social advantage. The use of common cultural identification for purposes of coordination is the key to culture's first face, and in southwestern Nigeria Yoruba subtribes so coordinated, but not Yoruba religious groups. As for culture's second face, my research showed the religious beliefs did not infuse Yoruba behavior outside the realm of religion, but (while presumably, though not directly investigated) ancestral city values did.

The study conjectured that a hegemonic state (in this case imperial Britain), through granting special access to petitioning groups, powerfully influenced the dimension that became socially and politically salient. Due to the flexibility of Britain's system of indirect rule, ancestral city became the salient cultural dimension in Nigeria's south, but religion became the salient dimension in Nigeria's north. As a consequence, religious culture had no discernible spillover into the political realm while subtribal culture did. Culture drives political behavior, but only when a particular cultural dimension is seen as politically relevant.

Cultural analysts could no longer link values and beliefs to behavior without knowing which aspect of cultural identity was the one on which people conditioned their behavior. Recent research reveals that group demography is the clue. In any society, if you compare any two dimensions (e.g. tribe and religion in Nigeria), the set of people who are in the largest category on each dimension (Hausas and Muslims) are called 'cultural pivots'. They will 'choose' the dimension (i.e. activate politically as a member of the category group on the preferred dimension) that gives them the optimal political returns—for example, in a poor country with government pork the most valued good, pivots will choose the dimension in which their category has the smaller overall population (in Nigeria, this would be Hausa) because each person in the winning coalition, if pork is divided equally, will get more of it.[65]

THE PERSISTENCE OF CULTURAL EQUILIBRIA

If culture is an equilibrium—as argued in this chapter—we should think of the degree of ethnic heterogeneity in any country (measured by the ELF score) as a parameter, that is an unchanging factor that is part of the understood rules of the game. However, as the tipping models of Chapter 2 demonstrate, ELF changes through such processes as assimilation and differentiation. In such models, ELF is not a parameter but a variable, a factor that is endogenous to political processes.

Thus an apparent contradiction. The cultural config-uration of the population living within the borders of a state can be considered a parameter—people condition their behavior on its permanence, as did President Siyaad in regard to the caste system in Somalia. It can also be considered a variable. In the Somali civil war in the 1980s, leading to the de facto separation of the former British Somaliland, members of the dominant clan in the separ-atist territory (the Isaaqs) who once were ardent Somali nationalists increasingly emphasized that they were cultur-ally distinct from other Somali clans, for example in regard to religious heritage. Other clans followed suit.[66] In a period of a generation, Somalia changed from an ethnically homogeneous country to one in which the population saw itself as nationally heterogeneous.

With such contradictions in mind, Greif and I have conceptualized ELF as a *quasi-parameter*. We argue that cultural equilibria are by definition self-enforcing—that is, no one has an incentive individually to change it. But over time, under certain institutional settings, the parameters supporting a cultural equilibrium can systematically change. Indeed, this is what occurred, as is shown in Chapter 4, in historical cases of nation-building. Bretons, Catalans, Alsatians, and other nationalities living within today's hexagon became French. We can say that ELF in nineteenth century France was self-enforcing but not self-reinforcing.[67] However, in other institutional settings, even with nation-building projects, ELF scores representing heterogeneity have been sustained over long periods.[68]

CONCLUSION

The coordination issues of language, as discussed in Chapter 2, do not rule out that cultural equilibria embed worldviews. Languages (and other cultural categories) reproduce practices that reflect common knowledge beliefs and points of concern. It is for this reason that culture is 'Janus-faced'. On the one face, culture provides symbolic resources that permit coordination and control; on the other face, culture embeds common knowledge beliefs that are transmitted across generations. To go back to my initial example, Somali cultural beliefs about the personal worth of people born from certain descent groups provided an opportunity for a dictator to coordinate expectations in his officer corps so as to protect himself from a *coup d'état*. Here both beliefs and common knowledge about those beliefs, both part of a cultural equilibrium, help explain political behavior. But as we have seen, common knowledge beliefs are not neutral about appropriate action. Languages embed within them appropriate ways to address conflictual issues—it seemed normal for Somalis speaking Somali to condition behavior on substantive criteria but when speaking English to condition behavior on procedural criteria.

Nations that are commensurate with state boundaries have populations that share common knowledge and points of concern. No wonder the nation-state model has been attractive to political visionaries. But, as we shall see in Chapter 4, that model is historically defunct. The political implications of the demise of the nation-state model are the subject of Chapter 5.

CHAPTER 4

Nations and the Twenty-First Century State

'In the systems of the last century, the "actor in history" has been the nation. . . .'

Ernst B. Haas in *Beyond the Nation-State*

SINCE the mid-nineteenth century, the idea that the boundaries of the nation and the state should be commensurate became increasingly accepted across the political spectrum and all regions of the world. In the mid-nineteenth century the German romantics saw the reconciliation of the state and nation as the fulfillment of a natural historical process. After World War I, US President Woodrow Wilson saw the equation of state and nation as the key to democracy and peace. And after the Russian civil war of 1917–23, the Communist victors saw recognition of national republics as a necessary step on the route to communism. In the waning moments of World War II, the national project was central to anticolonial mobilization in South Asia and subsequently Africa. The easy spread of the nationalist ideal in quite different historical and geographical circumstances is in part what Benedict Anderson in his celebrated treatise—and whose definition of the nation was referred to in Chapter 2—meant when he wrote about the 'modular' aspect of nationalism.[69]

The question for this chapter is whether there is a political logic that ensures the commensurability of nation and state. In other words, will multicultural states break up into their national components? The answer to this question is 'no'. Indeed, as will be seen from discussion of language rationalization politics in eighteenth century Spain, even the iconic cases of nation-states were not natural but rather built from heterogeneous populations. However natural these iconic nation-states came to be perceived, a new relationship between state and nation began forming in the second half of the twentieth century, one that sustains cultural heterogeneity. This point will become clear through an examination of language repertoires in today's India and the emerging European state (the EU). In the case of Europe, a formal model will show the equilibrium properties of layered cultural identities that will continue to exist within the boundaries of contemporary states. To be sure, in some cases in the post-Soviet world we can see a temporary return to the classic model. But the longer-term equilibrium is one that supports cultural heterogeneity within and across state boundaries.

THE EMERGENCE OF THE CLASSIC NATION-STATE

One of the core myths prevalent in successful nation-states is that these states are natural, in the sense of correctly encompassing well-defined nations within the boundaries of a recognized state. But as Ernest Renan made clear in his famous lecture on nationalism (see the epigraph in Chapter 2), these myths are sustained by collective amnesia. If the historic matching of the classical nation-state is only a myth, how did today's nation-states homogenize their populations in such a way as to give credence to this myth?

Spain and the Decree of the New Foundation

To answer this question, consider Spain, with a special focus on language diversity in the Catalan region. Catalonia, as described in Chapter 2, is a distinct and vibrant Mediterranean center going back to Roman times. It developed strong representative institutions in the fourteenth century, and its language and literature were well-developed at the time of the reconquest of the peninsula from Arab rule by the Catholic Monarchs that presaged a near 200-year reign by Habsburg monarchs (1504–1700). They signed chartering documents with Spain's regions (called *fueros*) that promised them local autonomy and the preservation of their ancient cultural rights. Still, there were collisions of wills between the Castilian center and Catalonia leading to a 1640 rebellion in which Catalan nobles joined with their rebellious peasants in a revolt against Madrid in alliance with the French king. In the peace treaty of 1659, portions of Catalonia were ceded to France, and in return France recognized Castilian control over the rest of Catalonia.

But Catalonia's position in Spain remained contested. A half-century later, in the War of Spanish Succession

(1702–13), Catalonia and Castile were again on opposing sides. The accession of the Castilian-supported pretender, Philip of Anjou (from the French Bourbon dynasty), to the Spanish throne has been portrayed as a final defeat for Catalan autonomy. Indeed by 1716 Philip issued the Decree of the New Foundation in which it was mandated that Castilian was to be the language of all judicial cases appealed to the king (i.e. *audiencia* cases) throughout the realm. A secret royal instruction that followed the decree urged regional administrators to do everything possible to introduce Castilian 'all around in a subtle way' that would not alert the population to the efforts. Catalan historiography marks this date as the 'end of the Catalan nation.'[70]

Historians have argued over how the Spanish state was able to create a Spanish-speaking nation. These historians point out that Philip and his successors provided some tasty carrots along with their coercive sticks. To be sure, the New Foundation Decree came at a time of cultural and economic ruin for Catalonia. But by 1778 King Carlos III permitted Catalan merchants to take part in the lucrative American trade; economic expansion for the Catalans reduced their anger due to the cultural oppression. Overall the period from 1730 to 1790 was one of prosperity, demographic growth, and bourgeois expansion in Catalonia, hardly a situation that demanded cultural resistance.

The major problem with the focus on the New Foundation as a turning point in the construction of a Spanish-language nation-state is that it romantically presents a picture of pre-Bourbon Catalonia as a unified society of happy peasants reciting Catalan poetry to each other. In fact, different social groups had quite different interests in the Catalan language, and the death knell to Catalan as a language of official life in Catalonia cannot be attributed to the Decree of the New Foundation. As far back as the sixteenth century, Jesuits in Catalonia began to write religious tracts in Spanish. At this time, an alliance between Catalan nobles and merchants seeking to capture some of the contracts from the newly enriched Spanish state—through its exploitation of silver in the New World—wrote eloquently *in Spanish* about their culture. A statistical analysis of *audiencia* cases from 1650 through 1750 shows that the shift from Catalan as the normal language of documentation to Castilian occurred a quarter century *before* the issue of the Decree on the New Foundation.[71]

What was the causal factor in this crucial step in making commensurate the boundaries of the Spanish nation and state? It was not a royal decree as Catalan historiography had insisted. Nor was it commerce, since the data of the seventeenth century show more commerce between France and Catalonia than Castile and Catalonia. If trade brings cultural mixing, Catalans should have moved to French rather than Spanish as their lingua franca. The factor that coincides with the switch from Catalan to Spanish in *audiencia* documents is the end of the war with France and the subsequent Treaty of the Pyrenees in 1659–60. After that war, many Catalan landholders sought payment from the Crown to cover rent for the quartering of Spanish troops and reimbursement for the extensive damage to Catalan landowners' property that ensued. To the extent that the king can decide whether such complaints are worthy, it made sense to plead in the language of the court. In this period, Catalan notaries advertised their services in preparing complaints in Spanish as a strategy for winning cases. The alliance of notaries and landlords suggests that a key to building national languages that grow to the size of the state is the control over legal judgments.

In the Spanish case, a central court created incentives for nationalities in the state's periphery to adjust their language repertoires (and their children's education) in favor of fluency in the language of the court. While haggling in markets could be accomplished with rudimentary pidgins, winning cases in courts of law required sophisticated language skills. In this case, a Spanish nation-state was expanded through law.

Other Classic Cases

France In 1539, King Francis I issued the Edict of Villers-Cotterêts, which established Francien, the dialect of Ile-de-France, as the only official language of the realm, replacing Latin. At that time many related dialects, such as Norman and Picard, had more literary prestige. German, Flemish, Catalan, and Basque and a variety of southern dialects (collectively called *la langue d'oc*) had substantial speech communities within France. Nothing was done to eliminate competing vernaculars because the Edict was not oriented at language homogeneity creating a nation, but rather to rationalize bureaucratic routines within a state.

It was not until the eighteenth century, and especially with the Jacobins in control over the revolutionary state, that the idea of a national language took on policy implications. Later on, under Napoleon, the rise of public education meant education in French. Nonetheless, French did not become the widespread national language it is today until the final third of the nineteenth century. As late as 1863, about a quarter of France's population spoke no French. It was public education, army conscription, and an attractive national economy centered in Paris (where jobs required speaking French) that created a French-speaking national culture up to the borders of the hexagon that was the French state.[72]

Japan Because of its geography and long-term insulation from foreign influence, Japan is often described as a *natural* nation-state. Yet even in Japan, regional dialects (*hogen*), at least until the age of mass media, were quite distinct. The four major *hogen* groups were those of eastern Japan (*kanto*), western Japan, Kyushu, and Ryukyu, each with subdialects. The Japanese Alps, dividing Japan east to west, helped to form and sustain the most politically significant dialect divisions.

Only with the Meiji period (1868–1912) did the notion arise of a standard Japanese language (*hyojungo*). The Meiji rulers, through national education programs, promoted this standard, based mainly on the Japanese spoken by one of Tokyo's middle-class speech communities (*yamanote*), which had been heavily influenced by the eastern dialect. This composite is known as *kyotsugo*.

The political organization of the Japanese state created conditions that encouraged young students from the regions to use *kyotsugo* and to rely less on their *hogen*. Japan's nation was therefore, at least in part, created politically by the state. The idea that Japan enjoyed a natural condition of homogeneity is not supported by its linguistic history.

In sum, the classic nation-states of Spain, France, and Japan show that policies of education, conscription, legal proceedings, and economic factors, such as attractiveness of industrial centers for internal migrants, were mechanisms that created the nations that in later years were seen as the natural complement to state boundaries.

THE POSTCOLONIAL STATE

Many of the postcolonial states in Africa and South Asia have been described as having arbitrary boundaries, not reflecting national cultures, and therefore somewhat suspect as nation-states. As should now be clear, from a cultural point of view, virtually all state boundaries are arbitrary. The question about the postcolonial states is not whether they were ill formed, but rather whether they (like their predecessors) will create unique national cultures within their boundaries. The answer is probably no. Due to distinct historical circumstances, many postcolonial states of the twentieth century will remain linguistically heterogeneous, typically having the contours of a 3 ± 1 language outcome.

A 3 ± 1 language outcome means that typical citizens of the country need 3 ± 1 languages in their language repertoires in order to enjoy a full range of services and mobility prospects within their country. Consider India, a federation of states each of which has a dominant national culture. At the All-Union level, English (the colonial

language, and the principal language of international business and higher education) and Hindi (the lingua franca
of northern India, derived from Sanskrit, the holy language of the Hindu religion, and an important language
in movies, news broadcasts, and other forms of popular
culture) share the status as 'link languages' used for All-
Union business and for business between the states and
the federal government. The Indian Constitution envis-
aged Hindi replacing English in this role, but this did not
happen as planned, in large part due to mobilization against
Hindi by English-educated Indians from the non-Hindi-
speaking south. In any event, all Indians seeking a range
of opportunities in their country need to have facility in
English and Hindi, making for two languages in standard
language repertoires.

Many of India's states give official status to their dominant regional cultures—for example, Bengali in West Ben-
gal, Kannada in Karnataka, and Gujarati in Gujarat state.
For Indians living in a state with an official state language,
primary education, street signage, documents, and forms
for official business such as health, contracts, and jobs in
the public sector operate in the official state language. This
is the third language that is part of the standard Indian
language repertoire.

What about the ±1? Indians who live in states where
Hindi is the state language (e.g. Bihar) need not learn
a third language to have a full range of mobility opportunities. They have $3 - 1$ languages in their repertoire.
Other Indians are culturally linked to states that have a state
language but are living as minorities in another state (e.g.
Marathi-speakers living in northern Karnataka). They are

protected by the Indian Constitution to have their primary education in Marathi, but also need to know Kannada to advance socially in their state. They have 3 + 1 languages (English, Hindi, and Kannada + Marathi) in their repertoires.

Is the 3 ± 1 outcome stable , or will it give way to consolidation around a single language as in the classic cases? Two historical factors have changed the fundamental logic of state building for twentieth century states, such that India is not on the course of Spain, or France, or Japan. The first factor concerns the role of language in governing a twentieth century state as opposed to a state that consolidated in an earlier era. In the early periods of state formation, states did not provide basic primary education, hospital care, and a range of social services. When rulers of these states issued decrees on language (such as the New Foundation), despite the King's admonition that the decree be implemented circumspectly, the great mass of the people was unaffected. If the state does not hire teachers, the language of the classroom is not an affair of state. But twentieth century states emerged in an era when states were expected to provide these services to all citizens—and thus the language of provision was an affair of the state. Homogenizing Spanish in the eighteenth century did not alter the expectations of ordinary citizens living on the Iberian peninsula; but attempts to homogenize South Asia with Hindi in the twentieth century had immediate implications for many, including non-Hindi-speaking Indians who expected to play managerial roles in state enterprises, qualified by their competence in English.

Second, postcolonial states came into independence with long-standing bureaucracies that operated in the colonial language. These bureaucracies provided job opportunities far more remunerative than in the private sector. Literacy in the colonial language was the key skill differentiating them from those unqualified to enter the civil service. Meanwhile, political parties were late-forming institutions, coming to existence when the colonial period was already in demise. When populist parties campaigned on issues such as nationalism, in the hope of ruling their countries through the medium of indigenous languages, they faced strong opposition from the better-entrenched bureaucrats, who feared their loss of status should civil services operate in national languages. Since populist leaders were weak compared to the bureaucrats who were formally charged with implementing policies of those leaders, it became clear to the new leaders that language reform would fail. A good example of this is in Sri Lanka, where in 1956 a populist party legislated the Sinhala Only Act—basically as a threat to Tamil-speaking bureaucrats who were overrepresented in the civil service—but found the policy undermined in part by Sinhala bureaucrats unwilling to implement the legislation.[73]

The inability to spread the plurality language throughout the country without facing repercussions from minority speakers (factor 1), and the inability to erase the colonial language from the bureaucracy (factor 2) worked together to give regional elites political space to promote state or regional languages. For these regional politicians, promotion of their languages would mean a protected civil service (in the region) where outsiders from the region could not compete for jobs, as they are not likely to speak the state language. This is the foundation for the three-language outcome, and there is no long-term process undermining it. While India is the purest case of the 3 ± 1 language outcome, variants of it can be seen in many postcolonial states of the twentieth century (e.g. Indonesia, Nigeria, the Democratic Republic of Congo, and Senegal).

THE EU AND THE EMERGENCE OF THE TWENTY-FIRST CENTURY STATE

To view the language outcome of the twentieth century state as having a stable multilingual structure is to provide a new understanding of the emergence of a united European state in the twenty-first century. It is commonly pointed out that because the EU will never look like France, it cannot become a state. This is a backward looking perspective. It is useful instead to point out that the state building process in the EU is more and more looking like that of India, and that therefore it is a harbinger of the twenty-first century multinational state.

In the emerging European state, English is the principal language of internationality communication and a necessary language for broader social mobility throughout Europe. Eurobarometer surveys show that even though there are more German native speakers than English in the EU, far more Europeans report knowing English than any other language. The European Commission reports that 83 percent of secondary school pupils in the EU are learning English. Even in Estonia, with many centuries of ties to Germany—it was colonized by Teutonic Knights as a reward for service in the Crusades—in a 1993 survey 90 percent of the Estonians answered that English was the most important language for business contacts, with German getting only 7.9 percent support. French and German governments can see the linguistic handwriting on the wall as they subsidize the learning of their languages across Europe, while British entrepreneurs derive considerable profit in selling teaching materials in English.

But the rise of English as a lingua franca has had no impact on the strength and vitality of the state languages in Europe. In all EU countries, children learn their national languages first and go to school where these languages remain the principal media of instruction. Newspapers, TV, leisure-time reading, advertising, and official state services all continue to operate (often solely) in the state languages. The EU has permitted member states to constrain by law the percentage of foreign language broadcasts available on national TV in a way to protect state languages. But this is hardly necessary, as citizens do not want their children to lose their national cultures. Bilingualism in Europe—with English and the state language—has become a norm. (The UK has the only highly educated monolinguals in today's EU members.)

Along with the bilingual repertoires that are now normal, there has been a new trend in support of within-state regional languages. In 1981, the European Parliament adopted the Arfé Resolution, which called for a charter for these regional languages, and a European Bureau for

Lesser Used Languages was established in Dublin. Languages such as Friulan (in Italy), Corsican (in France), Welsh (in the UK), and Catalan (in France and Spain) are now receiving subsidies from the EU for promotion in literature, primary education, and the media. In some regions such as Occitania in France, the promotion of these languages has a quixotic quality, more like a luxury item for upper-middle-class Europeans who want to preserve their ancestral pasts. In other regions, such as the Russian-speaking northeast of Estonia, or the Catalan region of Spain, there is a strong political interest among representatives of minority speakers in entering the EU as one of the multitudes of 'nations' rather than being represented as a minority region of a state.

As the power of the states diminishes with the growth of power in Brussels, there is a natural alliance between regional nationalists and Eurocrats to promote a plethora of micro-nations at the expense of the states. To the extent that this alliance succeeds, there will be EU support to get these languages institutionalized in local curricula. The EU will allow local politicians to use local language competence as a source of job protection (keeping outsiders who do not have facility in the local language from teaching and other service jobs). As a result, in some regions of Europe a three-language repertoire will become standard.

Thus the emerging European state will have a 2 ± 1 language constellation. Every socially mobile European (save for the British) needs to know two languages (the British $2 - 1$). And residents of Catalonia, Corsica, and regions with other minority languages will need to have facility in three languages $(2 + 1)$.

Is the European Constellation an Equilibrium?

An implication of the foregoing analysis is that highly skilled Europeans from the Netherlands, Sweden, and Denmark (just as examples) will spurn job opportunities abroad when their children are young, to ensure that they will get full literary and cultural educations in their mother tongues. But it is reasonable to ask whether states with layered linguistic identities can survive, or whether there is an inexorable logic toward the classical model where the boundaries of the nation evolve to make them commensurate with the boundaries of the state. To address this question, allow me to tell a just-so story of a non-EU member facing the same pull to English in its educational system. Consider a young married couple in Oslo, each of whom benefited from a world-class public education largely paid for through tax receipts from their parents' generation. They received through the Norwegian-linguistic-medium courses in literature and history, and increasingly through the English-medium technical courses in science and engineering. After graduation from higher education, they were free to explore the job market internationally. But after a few years, they plan a family. They want their children to be Norwegians in the sense of having language fluency, a deep knowledge of Norwegian literature and history, and a set of common experiences with other Norwegians of their cohort involving popular culture and events (political, social, and economic).

To be sure, Norwegian parents can instill Norwegianness in their children at home and through regular visits to the homeland during school vacations, as do hundreds of thousands of Turks living in Germany today. Public opinion surveys often show that diasporic communities are even more nationalist for their homelands than their compatriots who have never gone abroad. But as was indicated in Chapter 2, learning a language is more than the ability to produce grammatically correct sentences. It is to share the language's nuances among fellow members of a speech community. In interviews conducted among the Russian-speaking diaspora living in Brooklyn, New York in 2003–4, parents lamented that while their children spoke Russian, those who came to America before they were 8 years old were unable to fully understand the humor and the 'soul' of their mother tongue.[74] The desire that their children will have this understanding of their language and culture is the key assumption of my just-so story. Norwegians, once they have children, therefore decide to limit their next search to jobs that would optimize not only their expected life incomes but the Norwegian-ness of their children. In other words, national identification plays an important role in their job search with school-aged children on the horizon.

When people are willing to take paycuts to ensure that their children will learn their ancestral language and have easy access to others who share that language when they are shopping in the marriage market, they value nationalism. If the willingness to make sacrifices in the name of national reproduction is the fundamental criterion for the strength of nationalism, a formal model will show that nationalism should be greater in rich than poor countries. More provocatively, nationalism should be considered a 'consumption item' of the well-to-do. That is to say, we should see more of it as we get richer!

In the appendix to this chapter, I introduce a game played between a government of a country with a distinct language (say, Norway) and the set of its citizens who are highly educated and able to take advantage of the international high-wage labor market.[75] I call them Highly Educated Norwegians (HEN). The formal model assumes that language and its implications for the intergenerational transmission of national identities is an important factor in family choice. But as revealed in behavior, it is a factor that will be observed more readily for expatriates from small and rich countries than large and poor countries. In this sense, nationalism can be seen as a luxury good (a consumption item) for the rich. And as the world gets richer, we should thereby observe more local nationalism in linguistically distinct regions of the world. More important, an implication of the model is that cultural diversity will prosper if a European state comes into being.

The Post-Soviet Exception

In a remarkable shifting of linguistic tides, there is a discernible trend in the post-Soviet states for the sort of language rationalization that is typical of the classic state building nations.[76] In Georgia, Armenia, Azerbaijan, Moldova, Latvia, Estonia, and the Turkic-speaking republics of Central Asia, nationalizing states have emerged from the detritus of the Soviet Union. From the time of their language laws in 1988 (when they were still Union Republics of the USSR) to advance the role of the titular language (i.e. that language of the group after which the republic was named), newly emboldened parliamentarians in the republics have sought to make the boundaries of the republics commensurate with linguistic boundaries.

Historically, this has been made possible due to the Soviet policy going back to the 1930s of *korenizatsiia* (local rooting), in which the state promoted local languages in education and administration as a tool to promote universal socialism. Stalin, the expert on nationalism in the Communist Party of the Soviet Union, envisioned local rooting as a necessary step to win the hearts and minds of all the peoples of imperial Russia, on a long trek toward cultural merging and universal socialism. As part of the *korenizatsiia* program, regional languages (and publications) were subsidized, national academies were institutionalized, and national cultures were glorified. Although the full implementation of *korenizatsiia* was never completed, still by 1988–89 when nationalizing language laws were passed in most republics, there were cadres fluent in the titular language, and administrative dictionaries as well as educational curricula facilitating the governing of these republics without the need for the once cosmopolitan Russian language.

The fulfillment of the nationalizing program has been uneven but sufficient to create the foundation for a new set of classic nation-states. In Georgia and Kazakhstan, Russians have inexorably been moving from the republics, thereby lowering the percentage of citizens whose ancestral language is not the language of the titular population.[77] In Estonia and Latvia, as analyzed in Chapter 2, Russians have made efforts to have their children learn the state language such that they can assimilate into the new national culture. In Moldova and Azerbaijan, regions where minority languages were dominant seceded from these republics. Through these processes, post-Soviet states resemble the classic pattern of nations commensurate with state boundaries. They remain the great exception to the new twenty-first century multilingual states. But as these states become wealthier, they will serve as a new home to immigrants and their educated citizens will become more cosmopolitan. They might well be subject to the same pressures for layered identities that we see today in Norway.

CONCLUSION

In either case—the multicultural European and Indian states, or the neoclassical states of the former Soviet Union—national cultures are in formation, such that citizens from all corners of these emerging states recognize each other through a common language repertoire that they are fellow citizens. To be sure, it is possible that India and the EU are in early stages of national development and that rationalization of a single language will occur over the centuries. However, multilingualism is not only embedded in popular expectations as revealed in the HEN game but also in institutions such as the various Ministries of Education. Thus it is possible to think of a future India and Europe as both homogeneous locally (with a plethora of distinct local languages) and nationally (sharing in a language constellation) and through layered identities combining state-level multiculturalism with single cultures at the regional level.

The classical nation-state, one where a nation and state are commensurate, in which the national will is embodied in a state of its name, is today largely a nostalgic myth. To be sure, states have always bounded a congeries of nations. In past centuries (and in some interesting post-Soviet cases), there has been success through assimilation and migration to give some reality to a classical form of nation-state. But since the late twentieth century, new forms of culturally diverse states have been forming in which a complex set of languages (and cultures) prosper. Rather than trying to hold back history, a new political science should teach us how we can enrich public life through the adoption of political formulas that take advantage of the national diversity that exists and is likely to flourish within state boundaries.[78] An outline of a political theory to address such a political formula is the core theme of the final chapter of this book.

APPENDIX

A Model: Government and Its Highly Educated Population

The Provision of National Education in the National Language*

To give a formal representation of the logic as to why a multilingual Europe can be a stable outcome, consider a game (see Table 1) with two players, GON (Government of Norway) and HEN (a Highly Educated Norwegian).

* Thanks to Macartan Humphreys for technical help in simplifying the model and excellent guidance in working through its implications.

Table 1.

	HEN	
	Remain	Emigrate
GON		
Norwegian	v_N / $r - c$	0 / $-c$
English	v_E / r	0 / 0

The game

The game is played in two periods. In the first period, GON chooses between 'Norwegian' and 'English' as the language of instruction. In the second, HEN chooses to 'Remain' in Norway or to 'Emigrate' to the country that pays the highest wages for HEN's skills.

Utilities over these strategy combinations are as given in Table 1 where:

- v_N is HEN's utility for staying in Norway that is providing public instruction in Norwegian relative to emigrating. It captures both the income and the consumption value of the educational experience of HEN's children relative to what HEN would receive by taking the best offer overseas;
- v_E is HEN's utility for staying in an English instruction Norway relative to emigrating;
- r is the benefit to GON of retaining HEN in country;
- c is the cost to GON of keeping Norwegian as the language of instruction.

Two key assumptions lie behind the model. First it is assumed that $v_N > v_E$, that is that HEN prefers the reproduction of a national culture to the assimilation of international culture within Norway. This assumption underlies the support for retaining national languages. Second, it is assumed that $c > 0$, that is, given the size of its market, instruction in English is more efficient than developing curricular materials just for Norway. In making this assumption the deck is stacked *against* a multicultural Europe.

Solution to the game

To solve the game, let us look first to play in the second period.

Assuming that, when indifferent, HEN chooses to stay, then in the second period there are two cases to consider.

In case 1, in which GON chooses Norwegian, HEN chooses Remain if $v_N \geq 0$.

In case 2, in which GON chooses English, HEN chooses Remain if $v_E \geq 0$.

Since by assumption $v_N > v_E$, there are three cases of interest:

- case A: if $v_E \geq 0$ then HEN always remains no matter what the government does;
- case B: if $v_E < 0 \leq v_N$ then HEN remains if the government chooses Norwegian but leaves if the government chooses English;
- case C: if $v_N < 0$ then HEN always emigrates no matter what the government does.

Considering GON's first period strategy, given HEN's second period strategies (and assuming the government chooses English if indifferent), the government will choose English in cases A and C. In case B however, the government chooses Norwegian if and only if $r - c > 0$.

Therefore a Norwegian language equilibrium holds if and only if two conditions are satisfied:

(i) $v_E < 0 \leq v_N$
(ii) $r - c > 0$

Thus the Norwegian-language equilibrium obtains if and only if (i) HEN prefers a Norwegian-language Norway to emigration but prefers emigration to an English-language Norway and (ii) the tax benefit to GON of retaining HEN are greater than the productivity costs of sticking with a Norwegian-speaking curriculum.

Implications

- The protection of national languages and cultures may remain stable in Europe even though this may be costly to governments.

Ceteris paribus, retention of national languages is more likely if:

- v_E is low and v_N is high—that is, to the extent HENs prefer national language education for their children over a curriculum in Norway in which English is the medium of instruction. (This would partially fulfill condition (i).)
- r is high and c is low—that is, the tax returns to GON for retaining HEN are high while the costs of developing Norwegian language curricula are low. (This would fulfill condition (ii).)

Discussion points

1. To retain a skilled tax base, GON will want to increase v_N; government can do this through the attraction of foreign capital, which will occur if there is a strong ESL (English as a Second Language) program enabling foreign investors to operate in Norway with low transactions costs. Here HEN gets Norwegian medium of instruction and industry gets a skilled English-language workforce. (GON might prefer to increase v_E by so much that GON does not have to cave in on language. This would depend on GON's perceived cost of changing consumer preferences in the society for language.)
2. HENs remaining in Norway, having their children enculturated in a Norwegian curriculum will only be observed under conditions of high country wealth, that is, where the income differences between the best opportunity abroad versus the

best opportunity in Norway will be less than the premium for getting one's children educated in Norwegian.

3. Given implication no. 2, we should only observe the national language as medium of instruction in richer rather than poorer countries, that is in countries where the income differential between working abroad and working at home is the smallest. (In poorer countries where the national language is the medium of instruction, we would expect to see a growing private market providing English-medium instruction.)

4. *Ceteris paribus*, remaining abroad during child-rearing years is more likely the larger the sending country, because the larger the country (e.g. Germany or Japan), the more likely émigré parents can provide a reasonable substitute for national education (e.g. through schools providing education in the home language in major cities) abroad. Thus, long-term emigration is more likely for HENs from larger countries.

5. Protection of national languages would not necessarily be less in larger countries, however. First, for large countries v_N will be lower; but so too would v_E and this in some cases may render the threat to move credible, increasing the chances of national language instruction. Second, the benefits and costs of national language instruction might depend in other ways on country size. On the one hand, HEGs (Highly Educated Germans) will not have a fear of cultural extinction, and so no individual HEG would feel, by the logic of free riding, the need to pay for nationalism. On the other hand c, the marginal cost of producing educational material in German (as compared to Norwegian) will be lower, making the cost to the GOG (government of Germany) in providing German language education lower. Therefore, even if HEGs are more likely to spend child-rearing years in countries with the highest wages, this does not imply that the GOG is less likely than the GON to provide a German-language national curriculum.

Conclusion

This appendix has described a model (based on two reasonable assumptions) depicting a choice that educated citizens make in regard to their children's future in interaction with a choice that governments make in regard to public educational curricula. The model reveals an equilibrium in which the protection of national languages and cultures will remain stable in wealthy countries of the non-English-speaking world.

CHAPTER 5

Managing the Multinational State

'Our purpose is to consider what form of political association is the best possible... One of three alternatives
must be adopted. All the citizens must have all things
in common; or they must have nothing in common;
or they must have some things in common, and others
not.'

Aristotle in *Politics*

WHILE not a culprit in fostering violence, as we
saw in Chapter 1, there is a downside to cultural
diversity: it weakens the social solidarity necessary for a
healthy public life. This is sad news for those of us who
value diversity for its own sake, and for Aristotle who, in
response to the alternatives laid out in the epigraph, rejects
the Platonic ideal of the *polis* encompassing a population
sharing all things in common on more practical grounds.
But it is sad as well for those of us who project the demise
of the nation-state as the international norm. However
useful homogeneity might be to garner the goods that follow from social solidarity, the costs of eliminating diversity
through even peaceful forms of ethnic cleansing are high

especially in a democratic society. It is therefore imperative to find a route toward the management of diversity that does not compromise economic growth or the efficient production of public goods. After reckoning the costs of diversity, I propose a route to its management in this chapter. It has the added potential of enhancing democratic participation. It serves as a normative response to the political trends outlined in the previous chapters. While the route that I outline is designed for rich democratic states, I draw some implications of the proposal for poor countries that suffer from abysmal levels of public goods provision.

HETEROGENEITY AND PUBLIC GOODS

If culture is part of a coordinating equilibrium, what are the implications within the boundaries of a state (or a community) of cultural heterogeneity, where such coordination may be lacking? Recent research paints a troublesome picture. Cross-national statistical studies reveal a significant negative relationship between ethnic diversity and not only social solidarity (measured by state transfers from rich to poor) but also country wealth.[79] In the USA, there is a strong correlation between high cultural diversity in communities and lower levels of social trust.[80]

These results hold up even when research is done at the level of the community. Consider Miguel and Gugerty's study of Luos and Luhyias who live near Lake Victoria, in western Kenya. Due to British colonial policy there was considerable resettlement at the end of the nineteenth century. Some villages became homogeneous Luhyia, others became homogeneous Luo, and still others heterogeneous with lineages of both tribes. Due to the exogenously determined level of heterogeneity, having nothing to do with the kinds of people who were likely to move to heterogeneous or homogeneous communities, Miguel and Gugerty were able to identify the degree of tribal homogeneity as the source of the differential ability of communities to produce public goods. Two public goods were measured. First, they examined private contributions to the enrichment of public education, in what is known in Kenya as *harambee* schools. The central government only insufficiently supports basic education, so communities must contribute to get reasonable quality education for their children. Second, they examined community organizations to maintain fresh water wells that were contributed through foreign aid. In both of these cases, Miguel and Gugerty found that the homogeneous communities (whether Luo or Luhyia) were far more successful in enriching schools and maintaining wells than the heterogeneous communities.[81]

The causal mechanisms linking heterogeneity to slow economic growth and low level of public goods are not obvious. It could be that when citizens do not identify themselves with fellow citizens as *fellow citizens*, they are less likely to want to contribute to a public good that would be available to all citizens. Alternatively, it could be that cultural diversity makes communication difficult (e.g. the need for translators), and thereby the local community is technically less equipped to supply public goods. Finally, it could be that homogeneous communities develop effective policing technologies to assure each other that no member of the community is shirking in her or his duties to provide public goods. In-group policing can be done without danger; however, policing across cultural communities entails danger—for example, stratagems like humiliation of shirkers might be seen as a laughing matter (though effective in getting shirkers to contribute) among co-ethnics but as a personal threat across ethnic groups.[82] Experimental work in Uganda, in which subjects were paired (sometimes with their co-ethnics and sometimes with ethnic others) to solve common problems suggests that a sense of 'we-ness' as fellow tribesmen and the technology of communication both play less of a role than the influence on behavior due to in-group policing.[83] Whatever the exact mechanism, ethnic heterogeneity has negative consequences for community welfare.

What are the implications of these findings for those involved in political movements to increase heterogeneity through the promotion of minority languages, for example through programs of bilingual education? Language rights advocates have pointed to data showing net benefits to such programs. Steven May, for example, emphasizes that the promotion of minority languages in schools has long-term benefits for students of minority backgrounds, both in wider educational attainment and in success in the future job market. He heaps scorn on the ideologues of New Zealand's English Only Movement, which he says 'stands in sharp contrast to the bulk of academic research on the topic which points strongly to the attested social and educational merits of learning in one's first language...'. Equally questionable, he continues, are the federally funded research studies that showed no educational gains for students enrolled in bilingual programs.

He counters these results with a study that has 183 control variables and interaction terms that show admirable success of these programs. There is, May notes, 'wide acknowledgment' of the quality of these results.[84] This is consistent with recent research showing the limits of English immersion educational programs in the USA.[85] Therefore, May argues, restoring the vitality of language communities helps make members of those communities better educated and more productive citizens—and this would constitute an argument for heterogeneity.

But the data are ambiguous. Consider the problem of selection bias. Are those students enrolled in bilingual programs more ambitious than the others, as with the case of many experimental programs? Or are they less ambitious, thrown into these programs by principals who want to keep the least able students out of the standard tracks? Unless we know the criteria of selection, we cannot assess the overall impact of these experimental programs on student performance. One US-based study addressing this and other methodological issues finds a small but significant *downward* effect of exposure to bilingual schools in retention and in salary ten years after the entry into a secondary school program. For these losses, the estimated annual additional cost per pupil of bilingual programs is $1,000.[86]

In this light, note that in May's book we learn that the popular Kura Kaupapa (the Maori-language-medium primary schools), as with the case of bilingual US schools, do not give any added educational value to Maoris in comparison with those who enter directly into the English system.[87] So for uncertain gains at best (and losses at worst), taxpayers are being asked to provide extra funds for curricula that help sustain or rebuild language communities.

Heterogeneity is associated with poor public services and low economic growth. Attempts to achieve justice through revival of long lost heterogeneity are costly and yet provide little if any economic advancement to those who are targeted by linguistic revival programs. How can the burden of heterogeneity be lightened?

THE CHALLENGE OF MULTICULTURALISM

Whatever the costs of cultural heterogeneity, the costs of eliminating heterogeneity (as least in the short term) are surely higher, given the extraordinary levels of migration and cultural mixing in our age.[88] It is therefore imperative to learn how best to overcome the negative consequences of heterogeneity without subjecting minorities to any form of ethnic cleansing or coerced assimilation. In this section, I address some normative issues that follow from an acknowledgement that there may be costs to pay in the recognition or even promotion of diversity. I offer (based on a collaboration with Rob Reich)[89] a liberal democratic argument for multiculturalism, and suggest how the expected losses in public goods that would follow from a multicultural politics can be mitigated through the identification and the consolidation of ethnically distinct local communities within larger society. As an added bonus, the acceptance of a multicultural political agenda enriches our public sphere, which in itself is a democratic achievement.

If the opportunity costs of heterogeneity are high in the loss of potential public goods, the costs of eliminating it need to be reckoned. The problem with seeking to enforce linguistic homogeneity to promote the production of public goods is that there is no criterion to decide which language should be the preferred one in any community. There are two proposed criteria. The first is to say that linguistic justice is on the side of the winners. Take Wales. Brian Barry, in a polemical masterpiece, insists that the past is past, and everyone in that region of the UK now speaks English. Why promote diversity and pay all the costs for diversity (in terms of lost social programs) to revive a defunct language? Language choice, Barry claims (incorrectly as we saw), is no different from choosing which side of the road to drive on, and it should therefore make no difference to those whose ancestors are Welsh if they speak English today.[90] This appears to be a perspective held by the winners in cultural imposition, more or less in the way Thrasymachus argued (rather unsuccessfully) to Socrates in Plato's *Republic* that the meaning of justice is that which is in the interest of the powerful.

The second criterion is based on compensatory justice. From this perspective, we need to compute the costs to minority communities of adjusting to a common language regime as determined by the majority.[91] Intriguing methods of computing costs and awarding transfers to encourage families to assimilate have been proposed. However, in many cases of heterogeneity, even the suggestion of a bribe to compensate for abandoning an ancestral language is seen as provocative and threatening. In a series of interviews in Ghana, Ewe-speakers from the east were appalled and aroused by the suggestion that they might abandon Ewe in favor of any dialect of Akan, Ghana's plurality language-family. One respondent blurted out that 'you just can't kill one language and use it as manure for another'. Compensatory schemes may therefore provoke animosity rather than add to trust.[92]

These two criteria are costly each in its own way—the first denies justice; the second denies voice.

Suppose, as an alternative, we were to allow democratic politics to play itself out, permitting groups (as with the Flemish in Belgium, the French-speakers in Quebec, the Catalan-speakers in Spain, and Russian-speakers in Ukraine) to carve out administrative zones where their languages (and cultures) could be homogeneous, while at the same time living in countries where a dominant language compels them to be bilingual. That this can be done fairly is the core intuition behind the liberal democratic approach to linguistic justice. Such an approach should move societies not to a generalized homogeneity, but rather toward administrative zones within states of linguistic homogeneity.

This outcome, however, cannot be imposed by some distinction between worthy societal cultures (all of which must get their autonomies) and unworthy immigrant cultures (which get less-valued payoffs).[93] The liberal democratic approach views the resolution of many questions and problems of linguistic justice as the proper subject of the messy contestation of democratic politics rather than as the result of clean specifications from first principles that we observe especially in the compensatory scheme. In opposition to liberal theorists who defend principles of allocation based on assumptions about what people would choose if they had no inkling of where they would be placed in the social hierarchy, we believe that a vibrant democratic society requires a large area of indeterminacy in which liberal principles offer no clear prescriptions. Cultural issues in general, and language issues in particular, offer such an area that democrats should embrace.[94]

A liberal democratic approach views any citizen or set of citizens in a state as possessing the right to mobilize support for a language community or language policies that it considers a collective or public good. All citizens have an equal right to exert electoral or interest group pressure, to foster broader coalitions, and to engage the wider polity through democratic deliberation in the quest to provide this collective or public good. They should be constrained in these efforts only by the liberal requirement that the fundamental rights of all citizens not be violated.

This liberal democratic approach confirms the relevance of seeing the construction of a viable language community—as was illustrated in the case of Norway in the appendix to Chapter 4 and developed by Tamir in regard to nationalism more generally—as a consumption item.[95] Indeed, following from their right to vote, all members of a community must help pay for public goods that are democratically purchased. If a political unit within a state votes to have a once marginalized language treated as an official one within the boundaries of its local polity—a form of a public good in that it promotes local homogeneity—all taxpayers within that new zone assume a responsibility to provide for it. The bonus is the possibility of greater quality overall of local public goods provision, though at a cost of reduced state-level solidarity.

The right of a community to tax its members to create a language community as a public good implies for democratic liberals the right to reverse course and to let the language fall into public desuetude—thereby creating a larger unit of linguistic homogeneity. Tamir raises the case of Hebrew in Israel. In the period of early Israeli statehood, it was considered betrayal by many Zionists to speak a language other than Hebrew, but in the 1970s Israelis began to feel secure enough as a nationality to allow for an infusion of English into their culture.[96] Suppose Israelis, who were so adamant a half-century ago about the privileged status of Hebrew for their state, agreed to allow English (or for that matter, Arabic, or Russian, or Yiddish) to become the standard medium of instruction in Israel as is Hebrew today. This would reflect a change in the culture of the state and the self-understanding of that culture by its citizens. Tamir would respect this changed conception, even if she prefers an Israeli society in which all future generations rely principally on Hebrew. In this hypothetical case, local heterogeneity might be the result, and people would be paying for one public good (recognition of minority languages) with the lost opportunities of high provisions of other public goods in other realms due to the very heterogeneity they sought to encourage.

In a similar vein, Carens raises the possibility that immigrants into Quebec, who learn French and earn citizenship, might vote to undermine the very language laws that paved the way to their cultural integration into Quebec. As citizens of Quebec, Carens argues, immigrants would have an equal right to define Quebec's future as those with deeper roots. If not, then there would be unjustifiable classes of citizenship.[97] In this case, if they vote for English, they would be enhancing Canadian and even continental homogeneity. Unlike committed nationalists, democratic liberals make no presumptions as to the language interests of the citizenry. This implies that they would be open to changes in those interests over time, and would leave ample room for democratic *dis*agreement both between and within cultural groups concerning the best language policies. If people want to *pay* the costs of heterogeneity— seen here as a consumption item, and paid for in part through the loss of other public goods—that is a democratic right.

This liberal democratic view, unlike that of nationalists who see language protection as an inherent right,[98] is that the consumption of a language community as a public good requires no philosophical defense. In the abstract, the construction of a new language community or the reconstruction of a formerly oppressed language community ought to be viewed in a morally neutral way. It is a public good, like promoting the arts, or the opera, or a local stadium to house a professional sports team. Communities should be free to provide the public goods its taxpayers demand just so long as fundamental liberal principles are not violated.

To be sure, language issues are not the moral equivalent of preferences about sports stadiums. Some theorists in the liberal tradition differentiate constitutive from consumptive markers of identity, with the former outside the realm of choice. Tamir, for instance, argues that cultural choices are 'constitutive' and they therefore take 'priority over a choice of restaurant . . . [or] a specific make of car'.[99] And thus, language is sometimes coded as a constitutive marker of identity, and consequently of greater import than arts or sports promotion. But this presents no problem for liberal democrats. They could easily agree that language policies are not on a moral or political par with culinary, automotive, or artistic options, yet without requiring that we give preeminence to such constitutive identity markers.[100] In fact, liberal democrats are not diminishing a language's value to its speakers by challenging this rigid distinction between constitutive and consumptive markers, and claiming that a language community is a consumption item. The value of one's ancestral language may be deep, but that value is best revealed through cultural, social, and ultimately political action.

The revelation of preferences though action will show that different dimensions of one's identity will be central for different people: for some, it may be religion; for others, it may be gender, nationalist allegiances, or a sports team. Once again, the forum of democratic politics should allow the intensity of individual preferences to be registered in a way that reflects the centrality of certain markers in popular consciousness. If language issues register strongly, the democratic expression of these views conveys their importance widely within the public realm. And the need for citizens to articulate the public goods implications of recreating a language community almost necessarily draws people into democratic politics. The liberal democratic approach therefore provides greater space for democratic contestation than standard liberal approaches.

Liberals should applaud individuals who wish to rebuild language communities lost due to historical injustices. Perhaps liberals might even feel obligated to subsidize minority organizations representing peoples whose ancestors' languages were brutally repressed that are dedicated to the provision of a new public good. Moreover, liberals should have no qualms about the imposition of a local tax to pay for this public good, even if a minority within the taxpaying community does not want it. Indeed, the problem any polity faces is that for this public good to be achieved—as the tipping game in Chapter 2 highlighted— there needs to be a critical mass of speakers choosing that language within the boundaries of the community.

To achieve a critical mass of speakers to sustain a minority language in a region, it may be necessary to induce nonspeakers of the once-marginalized language to learn it, even if they prefer the *status quo ante*. It may also be necessary to demand that all government officials be able to offer public services in the once-marginalized language. This in effect creates a rent on wider society by speakers of the once-marginalized language. But as with any case of distribution in democratic societies, language politics will have both winners and losers. (We may not want a strong national defense, but we pay for it anyway, in accord with democratic principles.) These rents are not prima facie violations of liberal politics.

But liberal theory suggests limits to what a cadre of nationalist entrepreneurs can do in creating a language community. Without doubt, it would be outrageous for a community to prohibit use of the dominant state language (or any language) in private realms, just as it was illiberal for the Franco state to prohibit the private use of Catalan among Spanish citizens or for the Turkish state to outlaw the public use of Kurdish among its own citizens.

In aspects of both the Quebec and Catalan cases, liberal commitments to equal opportunity, not limited by the fortunes or misfortunes of birth, have been violated by overzealous nationalists. However, liberal *democrats* would expect political entrepreneurs representing minority language communities to use all available means to tip their communities such that it becomes normal to speak and write their language in schools and offices. A good example of the liberal democratic approach to linguistic justice is provided by the passage by the Catalan Autonomous government in Spain of the Linguistic Policy Act 1998. Through the Spanish Constitution, autonomous governments were permitted to promote regional languages as official within their autonomies. In the Law of Linguistic Normalization in 1983, the Catalan government legislated wide-ranging programs for the promotion of a Catalan language community within Catalonia. A series of decrees over the next fifteen years deepened this program. But fearful of its loss in a subsequent election, the nationalist party that led Catalonia throughout the post-Franco years (the CiU) sought to lock future governments (led by socialists who were less committed to the nationalist program) into the linguistic framework it had built. The 1998 Act was an attempt by the CiU coercively to commit future legislatures to fulfill the nationalist program of the sitting legislature.[101] This is democratic politics with a coercive face. The debates over this act, pitting those seeking individual rights for non-Catalan-speakers against those seeking remedial rights to the Catalan-speaking community for centuries of discrimination by the Spanish state, were filled with rancor. Partisans on both sides accused their opponents of bad faith. But all told, democratic procedures were followed, and both sides to the debate were constrained by liberal principles. Eventually the CiU proposal was passed by an overwhelming majority, including many legislators whose ancestry was not Catalan. Deliberation had therefore brought something approaching a consensus. Liberal democrats should applaud this form of politics, as it represents an appropriate political response to the fact of heterogeneity. Both sides presented what in Rawlsian terms would qualify as 'reasonable comprehensive doctrines', between which liberalism ought not take a side.[102]

Another borderline issue in Catalonia concerns laws that prohibit media of instruction in the dominant language for public education, while allowing it in the private realm. The law permits the rich to buy themselves out of the language regime (through private education in Spanish or English) while the poor are left with no choice (but to study in Catalan). Here is a case where the poor are paying the costs for fulfilling the national imaginings of the rich. This comes close to violating basic liberal principles.

Similarly in Quebec, liberal principles have been pushed to their limit in regard to language imposition. A law in Quebec uses criteria of ancestry, namely the territory of residence of the parents when enrolled in elementary school, to determine who has a right to opt out of the provincial language regime. For public education,

Quebec requires children of foreign-born citizens to attend French-medium schools while allowing others the option of attending English-medium schools. The original version passed by the provincial government was even more discriminatory. It limited the right to an English-medium education to those whose parents received one in Quebec, but the Canadian Supreme Court extended it to all of Canada. This rule perhaps violates a fundamental liberal principle treating people as individuals and not as members of predefined categories. However, Quebec nationalists respond that the opt-out for those whose parents studied in English in Canada is more liberal (in the sense of enhancing choice) than a blind policy that would allow no group to opt-out. Because it bordered on violating liberal principles, however, it was proper that the law be reviewed (and revised) by the courts.

One of the stickiest issues involving language and education concerns parental rights to further their nationalist goals through the education of their children. Suppose, for example, a family of anti-French separatists wants to home-school its children solely through the medium of Corsican. Liberals should oppose these private strategies based on the principle that all (future) citizens have the capacity to make critically informed choices about the lives they lead.[103] Liberals rightfully demand that autonomous persons must be capable of opting to lead lives different from those of their parents, and this is undermined through home-schooling curricula that are designed to provincialize the students.

A liberal democratic approach would therefore highlight two constraints on educational policy, one on the state and the other on parents. First, the state should have no requirement that children develop full facility in the dominant language of social, political, and economic life. Of course, there is a state interest in sufficient facility that all citizens can fulfill their obligations to the state, for example in military service or jury duty. But this does not demand that the state language be employed as the medium of instruction for all students, or even as a principal language for participation in political life. Perhaps a parent sees herself as a member of a diaspora, and seeks to prepare her child for a return to a homeland. Perhaps a parent is a regional separatist, and sees his own language as the language in which things *will* be done 'here' once separatism succeeds. Notions of a 'dominant' language, or a language in which, as Barry puts it, 'this is how things are done here', are conservative, and do not give citizens the right to invest in language repertoires that they think will best further their own future interests. Thus, though a liberal state may provide heavy incentives for learning the state language or languages, it should not require that all parents have their children develop native competence in the state language.

It might be objected that for schooling the future interest here belongs to the child. Indeed, it could well be argued, the state should prepare the child for citizenship in the political community in which the child is already a citizen. In this case, the state may have equal claim to represent the rights of its future citizens as do parents representing the present rights of their own children. Surely, it is in the interest of the state to promote language homogeneity through the imposition of an official language. But just as liberal democrats would give no special provenance to linguistic groups, the interests of the state are also secondary to and derivative from the interests of individuals who live within its boundaries.

Parallel to those against the state, there are liberal limits to parental discretion. What if parents educate their children solely in a language spoken by only a very tiny community of speakers? This violates the liberal principle of autonomy, and states should be empowered to constrain parents from so limiting their children's language repertoires. Parents should be compelled to provide linguistic repertoires to their children that allow them a meaningful range of choices as adults, for which speaking a language that allows a broad range of mobility and vocational opportunities is a sine qua non. Liberals should oppose any attempt by the some 4,500 speakers of Aranese (living in the Catalan autonomy of Spain) to restrict their children's language repertoire to Aran. Nothing in liberalism would demand that these children also learn Catalan (the language of the region), or Spanish (the language of the state), or French (the language of the neighboring state), or English (the language of the proto-European state). Liberalism and its concern for autonomy would require only that Aranese be complemented with at least one of these languages. Similarly with the Cree language community in North America. This language is spoken by about 45,000 people in Quebec, in Manitoba and as far south as Montana. Within Canada there are some local institutions that operate in Cree. Nonetheless, the range of mobility opportunities available to monolingual Crees is exceptionally limited. Liberalism and the demand for autonomy would not help us decide whether Cree parents should have their children learn French or English or both. But it would require at least one language of wider opportunity.

How can the sometimes conflicting goals of state and parent be reconciled, especially when either or both violate liberal principles? Absent the expression of a considered preference by an autonomous child, probably a teenager, on his or her preferred language repertoire, which the liberal state would be obliged to respect, there is no tidy resolution. The liberal democratic framework would require, both in these cases and in all other borderline cases that the conflict between the parents and the state be resolved through the courts or alternative democratic institutions that are designed to adjudicate fundamental principles. And this implies neither the liberal state nor parents have unconstrained rights to legislate the language repertoires of the children for whom they are jointly responsible.

Thus, though the liberal democratic approach provides much greater space than any of the other approaches for a wide range of permissible language policies, this space is not infinitely elastic. Both the state and organized groups of linguistic minorities are capable of passing through democratic means laws and propositions that violate liberal justice. Consider Proposition 227 in California, which mandated an extremely short transitional period from bilingual to all-English education. Suppose it were shown that such a scheme provided no academic foundation in the children's ancestral language and unnecessarily weakened their performance in the general curriculum? Is the liberal democratic approach too swayed by majority tyrannies? We think not. Injured parties should have recourse—and where that recourse should be depends crucially on the institutions of the country and the administrative level at which educational decisions are made—if liberal principles are being violated. If parents can show that the equal opportunity of their children to advance in wider society is constrained by democratically chosen restrictions, those restrictions should be overturned (e.g. by the courts) on liberal grounds.

If this approach successfully escapes the problem of majoritarian politics yielding illiberal outcomes, however, perhaps it is vulnerable to the charge that it depended on the prior and just resolution of boundaries within the liberal state. If a dominant national group is able to draw internal boundaries as it sees fit, then it will do so, frustrating always the attempts of linguistic minorities to secure a winning coalition for their political agendas. In his *Multicultural Citizenship*, Kymlicka insists that societal cultures each get territorial autonomy within legal boundaries. He suggests that liberal principles of justice can provide the parameters for boundary readjustment.[104]

But there are no liberal principles of cartography. As we know from a long history of such attempts to make nations commensurate with state boundaries, going back to Wilson's Fourteen Points, there is no cultural cartography divorced from politics that would satisfy such an aspiration. Populations and identities are too internally varied and mixed for such romantic projects to succeed. The most impressive attempt to reset internal state boundaries on rational criteria such that they would be commensurate with national boundaries was performed by Stalin in the Soviet Union.[105] The unintended results are instructive. Once national territories were provided with resources, groups that had previously seen themselves as culturally homogeneous split apart through the accentuation of minute cultural differences, with each demanding separate autonomies. Meanwhile groups given autonomous republics treated their own internal minorities far worse than had been the case under the previous regime. The irony is that this multicultural project was fostered by an appallingly illiberal regime.

There is a liberal democratic alternative to the expert setting of culturally based territorial boundaries. In a liberal democratic vision, a broad set of politically determined language policy outcomes can be equally consistent with liberal principles. Thus, internal boundaries ought to be open for change through political processes, subject to liberal constraints. Consider redistricting for Congress in the USA. Within limits, state legislatures that face reductions or enhancements of congressional districts alter boundaries on largely political criteria. More relevant for our concerns has been the creation of the Basque and Catalan autonomous regions in Spain. Basque nationalists considered Navarra to be a core province of Basque Country, but a referendum within Navarra showed the population to be against incorporation into a Basque autonomy. Similarly, Catalan nationalists argued that Valencian is a dialect of Catalan and that the province of Valencia should therefore be incorporated into the Catalan autonomous community. Valencianos voted no. So the boundaries of the two

principal autonomies of Spain were delimited by democratic politics. While the autonomists did not get all they
wanted, they each got a conjunction of willing provinces
to form an autonomous government within the Spanish
state. A final example is Canada, where democratic politics has determined (through referenda) that Quebec will
remain within the boundaries of Canada. These boundary
outcomes reflect the push and pull of those who want to
belong versus those who don't. Liberal democrats should
insist that boundary adjustments be part of acceptable
political demands, subject of course to the proviso that
fundamental civil and political rights are not violated. Any
group that sees an advantage for promoting its language
through boundary adjustment should be given access to
the variety of democratic mechanisms to press its claims in
the political realm.

The domains of 'justice' and 'politics' are not mutu-
ally exclusive. Liberal democrats need not decide, as a
matter of justice, what the precise boundaries of internal
subunits are before democratic politics can get off the
ground. Liberal principles of justice do indeed generate
certain moral and legal requirements that no democratically determined outcome should undermine or compromise. But, as Carens has put it, there is a difference
between what liberalism morally requires and what is
morally permissible under liberalism.[106] Liberal democracy
permits much more than what liberal democracy demands.
Within the wide range of morally permissible policies,
democratic processes are the proper institutional mechanisms for choosing among them and revisiting them over
time.

OBJECTIONS TO THE LIBERAL DEMOCRATIC APPROACH TO HETEROGENEITY

The liberal democratic approach to linguistic justice proposed here is open to a plethora of objections: it promotes Balkanization, thereby fostering ethnic tensions that could be avoided through residential integration; it will invite entrepreneurs from ever smaller ethnic groups to demand their autonomous region, eventually unraveling the state; while it may be appropriate to rich states that can contain diversity peacefully, it is dangerous in poor states where diversity can run amok; and that Balkanized autonomies can never live in harmony with the complex urban centers that are part and parcel of the world economy. These objections have merit, but the core principles of the liberal democratic approach remain attractive.

Balkanization and Increased Ethnic Tensions

It might be said that the liberal democratic approach to linguistic justice puts in place structural incentives toward territorial concentration of minorities. If so, does not the nurturing of such minorities lead to Balkanization and higher levels of ethnic tension, especially by 'sons-of-the-soil' who see themselves as owners of autonomous regions against outsiders who have not lived in these autonomies for generations? Indeed, it is true that the liberal democratic approach favors groups that are territorially compact, and it will, if groups organize successfully to create an administratively protected minority language community, sustain territorial concentration. While this might pose a danger to the integrity of the state, there is no liberal principle that compels national minorities to integrate socially with majorities in their nation-state. More important, the danger of 'sons-of-the-soil' violence reflects a state unable to protect the rights of citizens in zones where local majorities terrorize local minorities (who may be members of the dominant cultural group of the state). The solution to this problem is the establishment of a rule of law rather than the suppression of national aspirations.

Balkanized regions will put pressures on two sets of citizens with different implications for state protection. First are the ascribed members of the regional culture who refuse to take part in the cultural revival sought by the nationalists who mobilized in their name. This is the case of the many Basques living in *País Vasco* who want their children to study in Spanish and who have been terrorized for their views and actions in supporting a Spanish-dominant culture in their region. Here, the central state must protect minorities from the criminal acts perpetrated by cultural activists who claim to be their rightful representatives. Second are the outsiders to the regional culture who live in the newly granted autonomous region. They must either learn the regional language (as have the Castilian-speaking Andalucian migrants to Catalonia) or migrate to a more linguistically accommodating region (as have many Anglophones from Quebec who emigrated to Ontario).[107] Liberal ethnic cleansing, where those who lose local battles for culture move to more accommodating regions, need not have objectionable consequences. And homogeneity reached through the opening up of the political process yields not only enriched local public goods but also an enriched public sphere.[108]

The Inexorable Unraveling of the State

The success of any group through its coordinated choices in creating a new regional entity should, from a rationalist framework of analysis, induce new entrepreneurs to mobilize ever smaller cultural groups to reach the same level of coordinated behavior in order to get similar recognition. Something of this sort occurred in Nigeria. During the civil war (1967–70), President Gowon sought to defuse future conflicts that seemed naturally to follow in a country with three large regions, one of which was always outside the ruling coalition, and created twelve states, each with a capital and promised economic transfers from centrally collected oil revenues.

The prize of statehood was too great for ethnic entrepreneurs to ignore. Bowing to pressures from them, a variety of military-led governments further divided the country into 19 states and a federal capital territory (February 3, 1976), 21 states (September 23, 1987), 30 states (August 27, 1991), and 36 states (October 1, 1996). And there are ever new appeals for state status. The strategy of getting an autonomy and therefore resources for the group represented is equally effective in making demands for designation as a new local governing area—for just a single example, in the city of Warri a communal war has pitted the Itsekiris who have controlled the local government against the Ijaws and Urhobos, both of whom want the city divided such that each of these groups can have control over a federally dispensed local budget.[109] The best strategy for getting a federal transfer to your own group (and one with a reasonable degree of success) was through local rioting against the ethnic 'other' rather than through insurgency against the state.[110] The Nigerian story reveals the dangers of unraveling through the initial granting of autonomy to a few large nation-aspiring groups.

The danger of unraveling is, however, far less than the Nigerian example or that of Huntington's fears as expressed in his *Who Are We?*. In Nigeria, the oil economy, as has been documented more generally, atrophies the state making it unable to forestall the rapacious tactics of ethnic rent seekers.[111] But more generally, as was pointed out in Chapter 2 with de Swaan's floral model, the odds are against entrepreneurial success when it comes to the creation of autonomous cultural regions. Young people are attracted to cosmopolitan centers and will in most cases, especially if through liberal protections they cannot be incarcerated in their ancestral regions, migrate to those centers to equip themselves in the state's dominant culture. In the USA, for example, Spanish-speaking migrants, as Huntington acknowledges, have shown little interest in cultural autonomy, and have ignored entrepreneurs who have sought to mobilize them on such a platform.[112] In an open society, regional entrepreneurs have a tough task in provincializing the populations they seek to represent. Coordination to a new cultural equilibrium, even if the average payoff for members of a new regional polity would be higher, does not automatically follow from the admonitions of ambitious politicians.

Multiculturalism as Dangerous in Poor States

The justification for multiculturalism in this chapter was based on an assumption of a liberal democratic state able to enforce the rule of law. But Lagos is not Ottawa, and Darfur is not in Spain. Surely in poor undemocratic countries the danger of fractionalization is something to be reckoned with. Can the multinational state be viable in the context of poverty and/or authoritarianism? To this question, I give a qualified yes.

Ethnic fractionalization, and here the reader might look again at Figure 1.1 in Chapter 1, is associated with lower probabilities of civil war in poor states. The higher the percentage of the plurality group for states in the poorest of countries, the more likely it is to face a civil war onset! Heterogeneity poses no special danger, at least in the production of violence, for poor countries. Somalia is the perfect example of an impoverished country, plagued by civil war, and as ethnically homogeneous as any country on the African continent. South Africa since the end of apartheid has recognized cultural groups and granted them language rights, and has since been free from civil war violence. India, where the states are built on language zones, has not been without civil war violence. But the recognition of states based on language criteria—for example the creation of Andhra Pradesh in the 1950s—has tended to ameliorate violence rather than promoting it. In fact, mobilized demands for linguistic autonomy even in poor states have been the *least* violent form of ethnic protest.[113]

But there is a qualification. As reported, high levels of ethnic fractionalization are associated with low levels of economic growth. And poverty is linked to higher probabilities of civil war onset. It might therefore be inferred—though it has not yet been demonstrated—that fractionalization is an *indirect* cause of civil war, working through the poverty it cannot alleviate. But the 3 ± 1 language configuration that I have exalted in Chapter 4 may avoid the problems associated with ethnic fractionalization. After all, this configuration allows for higher levels of public goods provision (and presumably higher levels of growth) to the extent that the regional autonomies are themselves homogeneous. Local homogeneities in the context of state-level heterogeneity coincide with what Qian and Weingast have championed as 'market preserving federalism'.[114] That Karnataka (homeland of the Kannada-speaking Indians) can advance as the Silicon Valley of India induces other national homelands (as is the case with the Telugu-speaking majority in the economically miraculous Andhra Pradesh) to compete. While fractionalization may imperil growth, the amelioration of fractionalization through the promotion of cultural regions can, under certain conditions, foster it.

The Relationship of Regional Autonomies and Cosmopolitan Centers

A major objection to Balkanized multicultural societies is that they inevitably have complex heterogeneous urban centers, often seen by those living in homogeneous communities to be axes of evil. Yet these cities develop mechanisms of intercultural trust that allow their businesses to expand globally in a far more efficient way than integrated networks of ethnic brethren. In support of this point, consider Avner Greif's classic comparison of two early modern Mediterranean trade networks. The Maghribis were tight-knit and trusting, and only sent trusted agents on long-distance trade endeavors. The Genovese were individualistic and diverse. Instead of relying on relationships of trust to choose their agents, the Genovese paid their agents well enough such that absconding with their merchant's goods was less valuable than acting faithfully and getting rehired for another trip. While these two institutional solutions to the problem of agency were equally rational for the merchants, the historical record shows that when opportunities to expand internationally opened up, the Genovese (who could recruit broadly) but not the Maghribis (whose community was too small) were able to exploit them.[115] Diversity at the macro level when built on local homogeneities will allow us to be Maghribis in Utah but Genovese in New York.

The granting of autonomy to distinct cultural communities should, if the findings about heterogeneity are correct, promote the investment in local public goods. But for social solidarity and the enhancement of growth within the context of a single state, there cannot be a proliferation of regional languages with no points of contact. There needs to be layered identities, where members of all linguistically homogeneous communities share a national culture. In

Chapter 4, I already addressed how the 3 ± 1 language constellation makes this possible.

CONCLUSION

When cultural coordination succeeds, communities seem better able to coordinate on other things such as the production of public goods. Cultural coordination also plays a role in spurring economic progress.

The benefits of achieving full cultural coordination in a modern state, however, may not be worth the costs. As demonstrated in Chapter 1, homogeneity does not buy ethnic peace. If the danger of intercultural violence is low, then it seems reasonable to accommodate to multiculturalism rather than to eradicate it. And in this chapter, we have seen that there are benefits to recognizing and institutionalizing local cultural zones for democratic political life as well as fulfillment of popular dreams. This chapter has therefore proposed a liberal democratic mechanism for achieving local homogeneity. To be sure, liberal democratic practices will result in extralocal heterogeneity, but extralocal heterogeneity has its own potential payoffs.

Readers might have noted a tension throughout this book concerning the scope of state power. In regard to the taming of civil war violence in Chapter 1, the remedy proposed was a strong state, capable of effective counterinsurgency. In this chapter, the interests of the state are devalued in comparison to the mobilized activities of linguistic entrepreneurs seeking to Balkanize their state.

The key is a set of democratic institutions imbued with the rule of law such that these institutions are strengthened through participation rather than emasculated by it. These institutions can stand strong if society is built on a system of layered and overlapping linguistic repertories that create a new form of national homogeneity—a constellation of interlinked language repertoires rather than a shared single language.[116]

The time has come to think about nation-building in a fresh fashion. Nation-building, to go back to Renan's metaphor that served as the foil for Chapter 2 of this volume, is hardly a plebiscite, even if there is a strong element of individual choice involved in the creation of national identities. It is a process, as I analyzed in that chapter, which involves coordinated expectations. If the process is allowed to play itself out in a liberal democratic framework, we are likely to live in a world of cultural enclaves in states that are multicultural. This process may in the long term undermine the social solidarity necessary for the production of public goods and for the attainment of social and economic equality. However, as suggested in this final chapter, homogeneous islands with cosmopolitan centers have the capacity to engender growth that is beyond the grasp of isolated homogeneous communities. In any event, the alternatives—violent ethnic cleansing or even forced assimilation—are surely worse. This book therefore emphasizes the historically new problems in nation-building, and the challenge of doing so while recognizing the incentives for individuals to coordinate and ultimately to give loyalty to distinct nationality groups within their multinational states.

In the *Preface,* I warned the reader that the path from violence to the justification for multiculturalism would be complex. Indeed, the conclusions reached in this book, as noted with my appeal to Aristotle, are frustrating in that they provide no response to the problem of multiculturalism in which all values are maximized. However, I have sought to avoid one Aristotelian error—namely his assumption that the *polis* was the natural condition for human flourishing. The analysis herein does not, and we must not, build contemporary political theory on the defunct institutional foundation of the *nation-state.*

NOTES

1. Samuel Huntington (1996) *The Clash of Civilizations and the Remaking of World Order* (New York: Simon & Schuster), Michael Hechter (2000) *Containing Nationalism* (Oxford: Oxford University Press), and Stuart Kaufman (2001) *Modern Hatreds: The Symbolic Politics of Ethnic War* (Ithaca, NY: Cornell University Press).
2. Ernest Gellner (1983) *Nations and Nationalism* (Ithaca, NY: Cornell University Press), pp. 58–62.
3. Rogers Brubaker (1996) *Nationalism Reframed* (Cambridge: Cambridge University Press), chap. 3. In a later book (2006) *Nationalist Politics and Everyday Ethnicity in a Transylvanian Town* (Princeton, NJ: Princeton University Press), based on extensive field research in the Hungarian region of Romania, Brubaker undermines a popular impression that ethnic minorities living on the wrong side of the border are obsessed by their bad historical fate. In fact, their minority status is a small part of their everyday lives, and when it comes up, it is typically grist for joking rather than fighting mills.
4. Myron Weiner (1978) *Sons-of-the-soil* (Princeton, NJ: Princeton University Press).
5. Susan Olzak (1992) *The Dynamics of Ethnic Competition and Conflict* (Stanford, CA: Stanford University Press).
6. For another mechanism, see Amy Chua (2004) *World on Fire: How Exporting Free Market Democracy Breeds Ethnic Hatred and Global Instability* (New York: Random House).
7. The *locus classicus* of this argument in Clifford Geertz (1973) 'The Integrative Revolution: Primordial Sentiments and Civil Politics in the New States', in *Interpretation*

of Cultures (New York: Basic Books), ch. 10. On resentment see Donald L. Horowitz (1985) *Ethnic Groups in Conflict* (Berkeley, CA: University of California Press). The quote on group worth is from p. 143. On the symbolic transformation of ethnic difference into ethnic hatred, see Stuart J. Kaufman (2001) *Modern Hatreds: The Symbolic Politics of Ethnic War* (Ithaca, NY: Cornell University Press).

8. A comparable argument blames the Belgians for institutionalizing a racial division among the Hutus and Tutsis in Rwanda, helping to explain the 1974 genocide committed by Hutus. See Mahmood Mamdani (2001) *When Victims Become Killers* (Princeton, NJ: Princeton University Press).

9. On the guilt of the *raj*, see Francis Robinson (1974) *Separatism among Indian Muslims* (Cambridge: Cambridge University Press). On riot entrepreneurs, see Paul Brass (1997) *Theft of an Idol* (Princeton, NJ: Princeton University Press). On associations and the cauterization of violence, see Ashutosh Varshney (2002) *Ethnic Conflict and Civil Life* (New Haven, CI: Yale University Press). On the electoral sources of the violence, see Steven I. Wilkinson (2004) *Votes and Violence* (Cambridge: Cambridge University Press).

10. Data from Donald Morrison, Robert Mitchell, and John Paden (1989) *Black Africa: A Comparative Handbook* (New York: Paragon House). The definition is from p. 129. The compilation is available in Fearon and Laitin (1996).

11. Varshney (2002: 6–7) and Wilkinson (2004: 12–13).

12. In these calculations, I treated 'other' as a single category. Readers can log onto the CIA website [https://www.cia.gov/cia/publications/factbook/index.html], choose the country of their choice, and see how different countries compare using this algorithm. For an assessment of the ELF algorithm and examples of its use, see James D. Fearon (2003) 'Ethnic and Cultural Diversity by Country', *Journal of Economic Growth*, 8 (2): 195–222.

13. Fearon and Laitin (2003).

14. Sri Lanka experienced two rebellions instigated by the leftist JVP in 1971 and 1987, and a separatist rebellion led by the Tamil Tigers that reached civil war proportions in 1983.
15. Laitin (2001a).
16. Laitin (1998).
17. The web page of the Minorities at Risk project, housed at the University of Maryland, is http://www.cidcm. umd.edu/inscr/mar/. Fearon and I (1999) analyze these data on issues of group concentration. See also Fearon and Laitin (2001) for a fuller development of the 'sons-of-the-soil' argument. Laitin (2001b) describes the data showing the insignificance of language oppression as a predictor of violence.
18. Monica Toft (2003) *The Geography of Ethnic Violence: Identity, Interests, and Territory* (Princeton, NJ: Princeton University Press).
19. In the tradition set by Max Weber, the state is defined today as a permanent organization that is the ultimate provider of order within a geographically defined area.
20. This paragraph summarizes the statistical findings reported in Fearon and Laitin (2003).
21. James Fearon (1998) 'Commitment Problems and the Spread of Ethnic Conflict', in David A. Lake and Donald Rothchild (eds.), *The International Spread of Ethnic Conflict* (Princeton, NJ: Princeton University Press), pp. 107–26.
22. Laitin (1995a).
23. Laitin (1995a).
24. This is the image in many classic texts in political science, for example that of Alvin Rabushka and Kenneth Shepsle (1972) *Politics in Plural Societies* (Columbus, OH: Merrill).
25. Renan's theoretical position had a powerful contemporary political message: France's claim to Alsace-Lorraine (lost to Prussia in 1871) was a valid one, even if the majority of the population in those two provinces were

German-speakers. Scholarship on nationalism is no less immune from contemporary political debates, now centered on Zionism and its alternatives. I am part of a long line of Jewish scholars of nationalism—Hans Kohn, Ernest Gellner, Elie Kedourie, Eric Hobsbawm, Ernst Haas, Leah Greenfield, and Michael Hechter—whose ideal image of a political community is closer to late Habsburg Vienna and Prague than to contemporary Israel. All of us in this tradition have been seeking zones of security for cosmopolitans, those with a taste for diversity. Anthony Smith and Yael Tamir, both Jewish and with strong political attachments to nationalist claims including that of Zionism, are exceptions. Of course, the insights from this corpus on nationalism can be assessed independently of authorial preferences.

26. Eugen Weber (1976) *Peasants into Frenchmen* (Stanford, CA: Stanford University Press).

27. Abram de Swaan (1988) *In Care of the State* (New York: Oxford University Press), ch. 3.

28. Thomas Schelling (1978) *Micromotives and Macrobehavior* (New York: Norton).

29. Malcolm Gladwell (2000) *The Tipping Point* (New York: Little, Brown).

30. This example is from Gerry Mackie (1996) 'Ending Footbinding and Infibulation: A Convention Account', *American Sociological Review*, 61: 999–1017. Mackie's convention account is not without dispute. See Hill Gates (2001) 'Footloose in Fujian', *Comparative Studies in Society and History*, 43: 130–48.

31. On the parallels of cultural and biological inheritance, see R. Boyd and P. J. Richerson (1985) *Culture and the Evolutionary Process* (Chicago, IL: University of Chicago Press).

32. On attributes, categories, and dimensions as components of identity, see Kanchan Chandra and David Laitin (2002).

33. The payoff curves in Figures 2.2 and 2.3 are not linear, but this need not concern us here. For an explanation of the shape of these curves, see Laitin (1993).
34. This definition is only marginally different from that proposed by Ernst B. Haas (1964) *Beyond the Nation-State* (Stanford, CA: Stanford University Press), pp. 464–5, and that in Benedict Anderson's classic (1983) *Imagined Communities* (London: Verso). My definition highlights the political interactions *between* entrepreneurs and those whom they purport to represent, and *among* those who have coordinated beliefs of ethnic solidarity.
35. Laitin (1988).
36. The reversal of the Bourbon attempt to make Castilian the hegemonic language of Spain is more fully discussed in Laitin (1989*a*).
37. Laitin (2005).
38. See Laitin (1995*b*) for a fuller exposition of the assimilation problem for marginals.
39. Ernest Gellner (1983) *Nations and Nationalism* (Ithaca, NY: Cornell University Press), ch. 6.
40. Roger Petersen (1989) 'Rationality, Ethnicity and Military Enlistment', *Social Science Information*, 28(3): 563–98.
41. Laitin (1989*b*).
42. Laitin (1994).
43. Russell Hardin (1995) *One For All: The Logic of Group Conflict* (Princeton, NJ: Princeton University Press), ch. 7.
44. In Laitin (1991), analogizing from international trade theory, I refer to elites from the periphery as 'most favored lords' when they are given status in central society comparable to what they received in their regions.
45. On Israel, see Ian Lustick (1980) *Arabs in the Jewish State* (Austin, TX: University of Texas Press); on Germany, see Zygmunt Bauman (1988) 'Exit Visas and Entry Tickets: Paradoxes of Jewish Assimilation', *Telos*, 77: 45–77.
46. In Laitin (1997), I explore other elements, including religious belief and popular culture, of national construction.

In Chapter 3, I treat common knowledge of social status as an element of culture. But in this book, and through much of my own research on culture, the emphasis is on language.

47. I developed this approach in collaboration with Barry Weingast. See Laitin and Weingast (2006).

48. The anthropological literature on culture is almost synonymous with American anthropology for the past century. (British anthropology has had a more 'social' foundation, in which 'culture' has played a more limited role). Clifford Geertz's collection of essays, *The Interpretation of Cultures* (New York: Basic Books, 1973), is the classic text on the contemporary rebirth of cultural studies in anthropology, and relies on the 'web' metaphor. See Anne Norton (2004) *95 Theses on Politics, Culture, and Method* (New Haven, CT: Yale University Press) for the view that culture is a 'matrix', more or less coloring all aspects of our lives. In philosophy, that there is in any society a 'web of belief' that can serve as a foundation for the agreement on simple observation sentences—a lot less than overall visions of the world—as proposed by W. V. Quine and J. S. Ullian, has been seriously challenged. See e.g. Li Ding and Timothy Finin, 'Weaving the Web of Belief into the Semantic Web', http://ebiquity.umbc.edu/_file_directory_/papers/74.pdf# search=%22Quine%20%22web%20of%20belief%22%22, downloaded October 12, 2006.

49. This discussion borrows from Laitin and Weingast (2006) and from my fieldwork in Somalia. On General Samantar, see Laitin and Samatar (1987).

50. The Somali rendition of socialism—*hantiwadaag*—was literally 'livestock sharing'. This raised some eyebrows in the nomadic sector as herders wondered with whom they would be sharing their camels. See Laitin (1979).

51. Refer to the definition of the nation in Chapter 2. One of the key common knowledge beliefs are the rules, not

always internally imposed, of what attributes qualify people for membership in a cultural category (descent through the maternal line for Jews; baptism for Catholics; any blood tie to someone of African descent for an African-American).

52. Michael Suk-Young Chwe (2001) *Rational Ritual: Culture, Coordination, and Common Knowledge* (Princeton, NJ: Princeton University Press).

53. Avner Greif (1994) 'Cultural Beliefs and the Organization of Society: A Historical and Theoretical Reflection on Collectivist and Individualist Societies', *Journal of Political Economy*, 102: 912–50.

54. Greif and Laitin (2004).

55. For a promising approach along these lines, largely ignored by cultural anthropologists, see Robert Boyd and Peter J. Richerson (1985) *Culture and the Evolutionary Process* (Chicago, IL: University of Chicago Press).

56. Max Weber ([1905] 1958) *The Protestant Ethic and the Spirit of Capitalism*, trans. Talcott Parsons (New York: Scribner's).

57. Margaret Mead (1930) *Coming of Age in Samoa* (New York: William Morrow) and Ruth Benedict (1946) *The Chrysanthemum and the Sword* (Boston, MA: Houghton Mifflin).

58. Whorf's writings are usefully compiled in John Carroll (ed.) (1956) *Language, Thought and Reality* (Cambridge, MA: MIT Press).

59. Laitin (1986).

60. Laitin (1977).

61. The 'K' in the figure refers to the maximum difference in pairs making each of the types of claims, and these maximal differences, using the Kolmogorov–Smirnov two-sample test that is sensitive to differences in central tendencies, are significant by conventional statistical standards.

62. Thomas Metzger (1977) *Escape from Predicament* (New York: Columbia University Press), p. 14.

63. Laitin (1986).

64. These expectations were in large part derived from the classic three-volume work of Marshall G. S. Hodgson (1974) *The Venture of Islam* (Chicago, IL: University of Chicago Press).
65. Daniel Posner (2005) *Institutions and Ethnic Politics in Africa* (Cambridge: Cambridge University Press).
66. Laitin (1983).
67. Greif and Laitin (2004).
68. See E. Weber (1976) for the classic depiction of this process in France. See Ian S. Lustick (1993) *Unsettled States, Disputed Lands* (Ithaca, NY: Cornell University Press) for an analysis of why the project to incorporate Algeria into the French nation failed.
69. See Benedict Anderson (1983) *Imagined Communities* (London: Verso), p. 66, where the early nationalist model, on which it was 'impossible to secure a patent', is portrayed as available for 'piracy'.
70. On the 'death' of the Catalan nation, see Sanpere de Miquel (1905) *Fin de la nación catalana*. On the 18th century prosperity, see Jaime Vicens Vives (1967) *Approaches to the History of Spain* (Berkeley, CA: University of California Press) and Pierre Vilar (1978) *Cataluña en la España moderna* (Barcelona: Editorial Crítica).
71. This political analysis of the New Foundation and its results is from Laitin, Solé, and Kalyvas (1994).
72. On the French language in France, see Eugen Weber (1976) *Peasants into Frenchmen* (Stanford, CA: Stanford University Press) and Michel de Certeau et al. (1975) *Une politique de la langue: la révolution française et les patois* (Paris: Gallimard).
73. Laitin (2000).
74. Laitin (2004).
75. For an earlier version of the model and a discussion of its broader implications, see Laitin (2006).
76. Laitin (1998: ch. 13).

77. In Kazakhstan, as is the case in many postcolonial states, Russian (the language of the former metropole) is the principal language of the educated and cosmopolitan Kazakh elite. While this suggests that Kazakhstan will have the sort of multilingual equilibrium I described for the postcolonial states, I suggest in Laitin (1998) that Kazakh cosmopolitan elites will eventually migrate to the former metropole rather than withstand the nationalizing policies of the Kazakhstani state.

78. Alberto Alesina and Enrico Spolaore (2003) *The Size of Nations* (Cambridge, MA: MIT Press) show that as threats of interstate war have declined, and with it the per capita costs of national defense, the costs for a region to separate from a state have consequently gone down. Therefore, regional claims to autonomy are less risky for taxpayers who might from their actions actually achieve independence. In equilibrium, by this model, as long as the threat of foreign invasion remains low, we should see the emergence of ever more autonomy movements in established states.

79. Alberto Alesina, Arnaud Devleeschauwer, William Easterly, Sergio Kurlat, and Romain Wacziarg (2003) 'Fractionalization', *Journal of Economic Growth*, 8: 155–94. The result is even stronger if a measure of cultural distance is added. See Klaus Desmet, Igancio Ortuño-Ortín, and Shlomo Weber (2006) 'Peripheral Linguistic Diversity and Redistribution', Brussels, Conference on 'Challenges of Multilingual Societies'.

80. Robert Putnam (2005) 'Can We Reconcile Community and Diversity?' Harvard University: Justice, Welfare and Economics Lecture, April 6, 2006.

81. Edward Miguel and Mary Kay Gugerty (2005) 'Eth. Diversity, Social Sanctions, and Public Goods in Kenya', *Journal of Public Economics*, 89: 325–68. See aslo Edward Miguel (2004) 'Tribe or Nation? Nation Building and

Public Goods in Kenya versus Tanzania', *World Politics*, 56 (3): 327–62 for relevant cross-country data.

82. Chrisopher Boehm (1994) *Blood Revenge: The Anthropology of Feuding in Montenegro and Other Tribal Societies* (Lawrence, KA: University Press of Kansas).

83. James Habyarimana, Macartan Humphries, Daniel Posner, and Jeremy Weinstein (2006) 'Why Does Ethnic Diversity Undermine Public Goods Provision? An Experimental Approach', manuscript.

84. Steven May (2001) *Language and Minority Rights* (Harlow, UK: Longman), p. 217.

85. Yuko Goto Butler, Jennifer Evelyn Orr, Michele Bousquet Gutiérrez, and Kenji Hakuta (2000) 'Inadequate Conclusions from an Inadequate Assessment: What Can SAT-9 Scores Tell Us about the Impact of Proposition 227 in California?', *Bilingual Research Journal*, 24: 1–2 (Winter & Spring).

86. Mark Hugo López (1996) 'The Educational and Labor Market Impacts of Bilingual Education in the Short and Long Run: Evidence from the National Education Longitudinal Study of 1988 and High School and Beyond', Department of Economics, Princeton University.

87. May (2001: 304).

88. This is the purpose of Samuel Huntington (2004) *Who Are We?* (New York: Simon & Schuster). His hope of retaining the Anglo-Saxon Protestant American culture, if it ever really existed in the coherent form he gives it, comes across as quixotic.

89. Laitin and Reich (2003). The 'we' in this section refers to our joint normative argument.

90. Brian Barry (2001) *Culture & Equality* (Cambridge, MA: Harvard University Press).

91. Philippe van Parijs (2002) 'Linguistic Justice', *Politics, Philosophy & Economics*, 1/1: 59–74.

92. Laitin (1994).

93. This is a somewhat caricatured version of Will Kymlicka's agenda-setting argument (1995) in *Multicultural Citizenship* (Oxford: Oxford University Press).

94. The *locus classicus* for the notion of choice under conditions of ignorance of where you will be situated socially in John Rawls (1971) *A Theory of Justice* (Cambridge, MA: Harvard University Press). See Yael Tamir (1993) *Liberal Nationalism* (Princeton, NJ: Princeton University Press) and Joseph Carens (2000) *Culture, Citizenship and Community* (Oxford: Oxford University Press) for the seeds of the more political argument we offer in this section.

95. Tamir (1993: 54).

96. Tamir (1993: 88).

97. Carens (2000: 132–3).

98. As is provided by Charles Taylor (1992) 'The Politics of Recognition', in Amy Gutmann (ed.), *Multiculturalism and the 'Politics of Recognition'* (Princeton, NJ: Princeton University Press).

99. Tamir (1993: 41).

100. Daniel M. Weinstock (2003) 'The Antinomies of Language Policy', in Will Kymlicka and Alan Patten (eds), *Language Rights and Political Theory* (Oxford: Oxford University Press).

101. See the analysis of this act in Josep Costa (2003) 'Catalan Linguistic Policy: Liberal Or Illiberal?', *Nations and Nationalism*, 9(3).

102. John Rawls (1993) *Political Liberalism* (New York: Columbia University Press), p. 61.

103. Rob Reich (2002) *Bridging Liberalism and Multiculturalism in American Education* (Chicago, IL: University of Chicago Press).

104. Kymlicka (1995: 112–13).

105. Lee Schwartz (1990) 'Regional Population Redistribution and National Homelands in the USSR', in Henry R. Huttenbach (ed.), *Soviet Nationality Policies: Ruling Ethnic*

Groups in the USSR (London: Mansell). There are exceptions to the objective delineation of republican boundaries in the Soviet Union, mostly in Central Asia. For these exceptions, see Laitin (1998).

106. Carens (2000: 6 ff.).

107. Stories of publicly outrageous behavior in regard to democratic language politics abound. The size of French vs. English letters on Québec signage created a public outpouring of conflicting views. The disposition of books to the French and Flemish sections of the now-split Louvain University in Belgium (in which multi-volume sets of classic works were divided, making both sets useless) had a depressing outcome.

108. Jürgen Habermas (1991) *The Structural Transformation of the Public Sphere* (Cambridge, MA: MIT Press).

109. *Vanguard* (September 13, 2003) 'Nigeria: Why Itsekiris Are Against Ibori's Peace Plan for Warri-Egbe'.

110. For example, see Charles Ozoemena (February 26, 2004) 'Agitation For Anioma State Hots Up', *Vanguard* (Nigeria); or *Weekly Trust* (September 20, 2003) 'Nigeria: Split of Kaduna State: a Worthy Cause?'

111. On oil weakening the state, see Terry Lynn Karl (1997) *The Paradox of Plenty: Oil Booms and Petro-States* (Berkeley, CA: University of California Press); on oil, state weakness, and susceptibility to civil war onset, see Fearon and Laitin (2003).

112. See Jack Citrin, Amy Lerman, Michael Murakani, and Kathryn Pearson (2007) 'Testing Huntington: Is Hispanic Immigration a Threat to American Identity?' *Perspectives on Politics*, 5: 31–48 for data *contra* Huntington showing the strong and persistent desires of American immigrants to adopt the cultural patterns of the dominant society.

113. Laitin (2001*b*).

114. Yingyi Qian and Barry Weingast (1997) 'Federalism as a Commitment to Preserving Market Incentives', *Journal of Economic Perspectives*, 11 (4): 83–92.

115. Avner Greif (1994) 'Cultural Beliefs and the Organization of Society: A Historical and Theoretical Reflection on Collectivist and Individualist Societies', *The Journal of Political Economy*, 102(5): 912–50.

116. On the notion of a language constellation, see Abram de Swaan (2001) *Words of the World* (Cambridge, UK: Polity Press).

REFERENCES TO AUTHOR'S OWN WORK

This book borrows extensively from work that I have published elsewhere. When this occurs, I do not provide full citations, as I do for other work, but only author(s) and year of publication. Below are the full references from my own work, some of it in collaboration, that form the research foundation for this book.

Brubaker, Rogers and David D. Laitin (1998). 'Ethnic and Nationalist Violence', *Annual Review of Sociology*, 24: 423–52.

Chandra, Kanchan and David D. Laitin (2002). 'A Framework for Thinking About Identity Change', Paper Prepared for Presentation at LICEP 5, Stanford University [http://www.yale.edu/ycias/ocvprogram/licep/5/chandra-laitin/chandra-laitin.pdf].

Fearon, James D. and David D. Laitin (1996). 'Explaining Interethnic Cooperation', *American Political Science Review*, 90(4): 715–35.

——— (1999). 'Weak States, Rough Terrain, And Large-Scale Ethnic Violence Since 1945', Paper prepared for delivery at the 1999 Annual Meetings of the American Political Science Association, 2–5 September, Atlanta, GA.

——— (2001). 'Sons of the Soil, Immigrants and Civil War', Stanford University, unpublished manuscript, http://www.stanford.edu/class/polisci313/papers/LaitinOct29.pdf

——— (2003). 'Ethnicity, Insurgency and Civil War', *American Political Science Review*, 97(1): 75–90.

——— (no date). 'Nigeria', in Random Narratives (http://www.stanford.edu / group / ethnic / Random%20Narratives / random%20narratives.htm).

Greif, Avner and David D. Laitin (2004). 'A Theory of Endogenous Institutional Change', *American Political Science Review*, 98(4): 633–52.

Laitin, David D. (1977). *Politics, Language, and Thought: The Somali Experience*. Chicago, IL: University of Chicago Press.

—— (1979). 'Somalia's Military Government and Scientific Socialism', in Thomas M. Callaghy and Carl G. Rosberg (eds), *Socialism in Sub-Saharan Africa*. Berkeley, CA: Institute of International Studies.

—— (1983). 'The Ogaadeen Question and Changes in Somali Identity', in Donald Rothchild and Victor A. Olorunsola (eds), *State Versus Ethnic Claims: African Policy Dilemmas*. Boulder, CO: Westview.

—— (1986). *Hegemony and Culture*. Chicago, IL: University of Chicago Press.

—— (1988). 'Language Games', *Comparative Politics*, 20: 289–302.

—— (1989a). 'Linguistic Revival: Politics and Culture in Catalonia', *Comparative Studies in Society and History*, 31(2): 297–317.

—— (1989b). 'Language Policy and Political Strategy in India', *Policy Sciences*, 22: 415–36.

—— (1991). 'The National Uprisings in the Soviet Union', *World Politics*, 44(1): 139–177.

—— (1992). *Language Repertoires and State Construction in Africa*. Cambridge: Cambridge University Press.

—— (1993). 'The Game Theory of Language Regimes', *International Political Science Review*, 14(3): 227–39.

—— (1994). 'The Tower of Babel as a Coordination Game: Political Linguistics in Ghana', *American Political Science Review*, 88(3): 622–34.

—— (Spring, 1995a). 'National Revivals and Violence', *Archives Européennes de Sociologie*.

—— (1995b). 'Marginality: A Microperspective', *Rationality and Society*, 7(1): 31–57.

_____ (1997). 'The Cultural Identities of a European State', *Politics & Society*, 25(3): 277–302.

_____ (1998). *Identity in Formation: The Russian-speaking Populations in the Near Abroad*. Ithaca, NY: Cornell University Press.

_____ (2000). 'Language Conflict and Violence: the Straw that Strengthens the Camel's Back', *Archives Européennes de Sociologie*, XLI (1): 97–137.

_____ (2001*a*). 'Secessionist Rebellion in the Former Soviet Union', *Comparative Political Studies*, 34(8): 839–61.

_____ (2001*b*). 'Language Conflict and Violence', *Archives Européennes de Sociologie*, 41 (1).

_____ (2004). 'The De-cosmopolitanization of the Russian Diaspora: A View from Brooklyn in the "Far Abroad"', *Diaspora: A Journal of Transnational Studies*, 13(1): 5–35.

_____ (2005). 'Culture Shift in a Postcommunist State', in Zoltan Barany and Robert G. Moser (eds.), *Ethnic Politics After Communism*. Ithaca, NY: Cornell University Press.

_____ (2006). 'Linguistic Nationalism as a Consumption Item', Paper presented at the conference on Challenges Of Multi-Lingual Societies, Organized by CORE, Université catholique de Louvain, and ECARES, Université Libre de Bruxelles (June 9–10, 2006).

_____ and Barry Weingast (2006). 'An Equilibrium Alternative to the Study of Culture', *The Good Society*, 15(1): 15–20.

_____ and Rob Reich (2003). 'A Liberal Democratic Approach to Language Justice', in Will Kymlicka and Alan Patten (eds.), *Language Rights and Political Theory*. Oxford: Oxford University Press.

_____ and Said S. Samatar (1987). *Somalia: A Nation in Search of a State*. Boulder, CO: Westview.

_____ Carlotta Solé, and Stathis N. Kalyvas (1994). 'Language and the Construction of States: The Case of Catalonia in Spain', *Politics & Society*, 22(1): 5–30.

INDEX

Alesina, Alberto 147
Anderson, Benedict 82, 143, 146
Aristotle ix, 107, 138
Armenia 5–6, 97
assimilation 77
    competitive 45–9
    openness to 18
Austria 3
Austro-Hungarian Empire 4
Azerbaijan 15, 16, 18, 97, 99

Balkanization 129–31
Bangladesh 7
Barry, Brian 113, 123, 148
battle of the sexes game 39–40
Bauman, Zygmunt 143
Benedict, Ruth 69–70, 145
Biafra 41
bilingualism 33, 112, 113
    education 110–11
    EU 93
    Somali students 71–4
    see also language; multilingualism
Boas, Franz 69
Boehm, Christopher 147
Boyd, Robert 142, 145
Brass, Paul 9, 140
Brubaker, Rogers 5, 139
Burma 7
Butler, Yuko Goto 148

Calvin 69
Canada 15
    NHL 35–6
    Quebec 116–17, 120–2, 128
Carens, Joseph 116, 128, 149
Carlos III, King of Spain 84

Carroll, John 145
Catalan Autonomous
    Government 44
    Linguistic Policy Act of 1998 120
Chandra, Kanchan 143
China 7, 36
Chua, Amy 139
Chwe, Michael Suk-Young 145
CIA Factbook 12, 13
Citrin, Jack 150
civil war 15–18, 21–2, 26, 133
collective consciousness 30
commitment problem 22
common knowledge 65, 66–7, 68
communalism 2, 7–9
communications difficulties 31–2,
    109
community boundaries 119, 126–8
compensatory justice 113
constitutive markers of
    identity 117–18
consumptive markers of
    identity 117–18
cooperation:
    ethnic vii, 10–11
    strategic viii
coordinated expectations 137
coordination:
    costs and benefits 136
    desire for 58
coordination game, pure 39
Costa, Josep 149
country size:
    and emigration 104
    and language protection 104
Crida a la Solidaridat (Catalan
    nationalist organization) 45

[157]

cultural beliefs 65
cultural groups *see* groups
cultural heterogeneity:
  costs of 113
  and public goods 108–12
  see also diversity; multiculturalism
cultural identities 40
  primordial 26
cultural pivots 76–7
culture:
  definition 64–8
  and economic behaviour 68–9
  equilibrium viii, 61, 62–8, 77–8
  as matrix 62–4
  points of concern 74
  transmission of 62, 68–74
Czechoslovak Republic 3, 5

Darfur 8
de Certeau, Michel 146
de Swaan, Abram 32–5, 53, 132, 142, 150
Desmet, Klaus 147
Devleeschauwer, Arnaud 147
Ding, Li 144
diversity 107–8
  and national wealth 108–10
  and trust 108
  see also cultural heterogeneity; multiculturalism

Easterly, William 147
ecological conditions 21
economic behaviour 68–9, 70–1, 74–6
economic growth 134
  see also national wealth
economic payoffs 53–5
education:
  bilingual 110–11
  effect on language survival 100–5
educational choice 38–9
emigration 104
entropy resistance (term coined by Ernest Gellner) 51

Estonia 15, 16, 24, 47–9, 93, 97, 98
Ethiopia 62–3
ethnic cooperation vii, 10–11
ethnic entrepreneurs 34, 37, 41, 131
ethnic fractionalization:
  and civil war 133
  and economic growth 134
Ethnic Linguistic Fractionalization (ELF) 12–15, 77–8
ethnicity, politics of 37
European Union (EU) 82
  bilingualism in 93
  lingua franca of 92–3
  as multinational state 92–9
  regional languages 93–4
  external homelands 3, 5

Fearon, James D. 140–1, 150
Ferdinand, King of Spain 42
Finin, Timothy 144
floral model of Abram de Swaan 32–5, 53, 132
foreign investment 103
France 78, 83, 85
  emergence of nation-state 86–7
  languages 32, 86–7, 93–4
  Third Republic 56–7
Francis I, King of France 86
Franco, General Francisco 43

game theoretic approach 66
Gates, Hill 142
Geertz, Clifford 140, 144
Gellner, Ernest 4, 51, 139, 142, 143
Genovese 135
Georgia 23, 97, 98
Germany 3, 5, 32, 57, 81, 93
Ghana 54, 113–14
Gladwell, Malcolm 36, 142
Gowon, Yakubu (President of Nigeria) 131
Greenfield, Leah 142
Greif, Avner 78, 135, 145, 146, 150

groups 64–5, 74
  concentration 19
  demography 76
  see also in-group; marginal groups;
    out-group
Gugerty, Mary Kay 147
Gutiérrez, Michele Bousquet 148
Gutmann, Amy 149

Haas, Ernst B. v, 81, 142, 143
Habermas, Jürgen 150
Habyarimana, James 148
Hakuta, Kenji 148
Hardin, Russell 56, 143
hatred 16, 18
Hechter, Michael 139, 142
Highly Educated Norwegian
  (HEN) 100–5
Hitler, Adolf (Chancellor of
  Germany) 1, 5
Hobsbawm, Eric 142
Hodgson, Marshall G. S. 146
Horowitz, Donald L. 8, 10, 15, 140
Hough, Jerry 16
Humphreys, Macartan 100, 148
Hungary 5, 52
Huntington, Samuel 132, 139, 148
Huttenbach, Henry R. 149

identity 59
  choice of 54, 58
  markers of 117–18
  national vii–viii, 30–1, 36–40, 49
  primordial 26
in-group:
  policing 10–11, 110
  status 55–6
  see also groups; marginal groups;
    out-group
India:
  Harijans 49, 52, 53, 54
  Hindu-Muslim conflict 7, 8–9,
    11
  Karnataka 134
  languages 54, 82, 88–90, 99, 133

indigenous populations 6
Indonesia 4, 7
intra-group killing 26
Iraq 8
Irish language 25
irredentism 2, 3, 5–6
Isabela (Queen of Spain) 42
Israel 57, 74, 116
Italy 3, 94

Japan 87–8
Jaume I (Count-King of
  Catalonia-Aragon) 42
Jews 49, 53, 57
job competition 7–8
job opportunities 95, 96

Kalyvas, Stathis 146
Karl, Terry Lynn 150
Kaufman, Stuart J. 139, 140
Kazakhstan 12–14, 15, 16, 98
Kedourie, Elie 142
Kenya 8, 41, 108–9
Kohn, Hans 142
Kurlat, Sergio 147
Kymlicka, Will 126, 148, 149

Laitin, David D. 141, 143–7, 148,
  150
Lake, David A. 141
language 31
  2 ± 1 outcome 94
  3 ± 1 outcome 88, 90–2, 134
  and behaviour 70–4, 78
  effect of education system 100–5
  imposed 121–2
  as cultural indicator 58–9
  minority 110–11
  outcome model 100–5
  protection 104
  and public goods 115–16
  rationalization of 97–9
  role in 20th century state 90–1
  shift models 32–6
  stable outcomes 95–7

language (*cont.*)
   and tipping game 37–9
   use prohibited 119–20
language entrepreneurs 46
language relativity theory 61
Latvia 15, 97, 98
Lerman, Amy 150
liberal democracy ix, 110, 112,
   114–35, 136–8
linguistic homogeneity 113, 136
linguistic justice 114–28
López, Mark Hugo 148
Lustick, Ian 143

Mackie, Gerry 142
Maghribis 135
Mali 7
Mamdani, Mahmood 140
marginal groups:
   continued existence of 49–53
   internal dynamics 52
   tipping game 50–1
   see also groups; in-group;
      out-group
May, Stephen 110–11, 148
Mead, Margaret 69, 145
Metzger, Thomas 74, 146
Miguel, Edward 108–9, 147
minorities:
   concentration of 129–30
   language 110–11
   national 4–5
Minorities at Risk data 18–19
Mitchell, Robert 140
Moldova 6, 15–16, 18, 24–5, 97,
   99
monopoly mediators (concept of
   Abram de Swaan) 33
Morrison, Donald 140
Moynihan, Daniel P. (US Senator
   and Ambassador to the UN) 1,
   2, 10, 11, 139
multiculturalism ix, 99
   challenge of 112–28
   and poverty 133–4

see also cultural heterogeneity;
   diversity
multilingualism 99
   see also bilingualism; language
Murakami, Michael 150

Napoleon Bonaparte (Emperor of
   France) 1, 86
nation:
   21st century 81–103
   defined 40–1
nation-building 29–30, 32, 137
nation-state, classic viii–ix, 82–8
national identity vii–viii
   measurement of 31
   and tipping game 36–40
national wealth 108–10
   see also economic growth
nationalism:
   as consumption item 97, 103–4,
      115–16
   dangers of 1
   of diasporic communities 96
   and violence 2–9
New Zealand 110–11
Nigeria 4, 8, 25
   civil war 131–2
   Yorubas in 74–6
Norton, Anne 144
Norway 56, 95, 99

Olzak, Susan 8, 139
openness to assimilation 18
Orr, Jennifer Evelyn 148
Ortuño-Ortín, Ignacio 147
Ottoman Empire 7
out-group:
   acceptance 56–7
   rejection 57
   see also groups; in-group; marginal
      groups
Ozoemena, Charles 150

Paden, John 140
Pakistan 7

Palestine 41
Papua New Guinea 7
parental rights 122–5
Patten, Alan 149
Pearson, Kathryn 150
Petersen, Roger 143
Philip of Anjou (first Bourbon King
    of Spain) 84
Philippines 7
Plato 113
plebiscite 30, 31
pogroms 7–9
political entrepreneurs 37, 42, 120
political parties 91
politics:
    democratic 118
    of ethnicity 37
    liberal democracy ix, 112,
        114–35, 136–8
Posner, Daniel 146, 148
postcolonial state 81, 88–92
poverty:
    and multiculturalism 133–4
    see also economic growth; national
        wealth
primordial identities 26
public goods 108–12, 115–16
Putnam, Robert 147

Qian, Yingyi 134, 150
Quine, W. V. 144

Rabushka, Alvin 141
rational choice model 49
Rawls, John 148, 149
regional cultures 41–5
Reich, Rob 112, 148, 149
religion 69–71, 74–6
Renan, Ernest 29–30, 31, 53, 57,
    83, 137, 142
resentment theory 15–16
Richerson, Peter J. 142, 145
Robinson, Francis 140
Roma 49, 53
Romania 5

Rothchild, Donald 141
Rousseau, J.-J. 30, 31
Russia 6, 7
Rwanda vii

Samantar, Maxamad Caali (Somali
    Minister of Defense) 63–5, 67,
    144
Samatar, Said S. 144
Samoa 69
Sanpere y Miquel, Salvador 146
Sapir, Edward 70
Schelling, Thomas 35–6, 59, 142
Schwartz, Lee 149
secession 2, 4–6
secessionist movements 25–6
selection bias 23, 24, 111
Senegal 8
Serbia 5
Shepsle, Kenneth 141
Siyaad, Maxamad Barre (Somali
    President) 62–4, 66–7, 77
Smith, Anthony 142
Socrates 113
Solé, Carlota 146
solidarity norms 52
Somalia 3, 8, 15, 133
    cultural equilibrium
        example 62–4, 67, 77–9
    language experiment 71–4
sons-of-the-soil 2, 6–7, 19–21, 129
South Africa 57, 133
Soviet Union 5, 23, 47, 55, 98, 127
Spain 4, 32, 82, 94
    Basque region of 23, 25, 56, 127,
        130
    Castilian-speakers in Catalan
        region of 46–7, 54
    Catalans in 42–5
    Catalonia 23, 83–6, 120–1, 127
    Decree of New Foundation
        84–5
    emergence of nation-state 83–6
    Treaty of Pyrenees 85
Spolaore, Enrico 147

Sri Lanka 4, 6, 12, 13, 20, 91
Stalin (Soviet leader), Joseph 29, 98, 127
Standard Average European (concept of Benjamin Lee Whorf) 70
state:
  boundaries within 126–8
  multinational 92–9
  postcolonial 81, 88–92
  scope of 136
  unravelling of 130–3
  versus parental rights 122–5
  weak 21–2
  see also nation
stigma 55
strategic separation 41–5
strategic stasis 49–53
Sudan vii, 8, 25
symbols, shared viii, 65

Tamir, Yael 115–16, 117, 142, 149
Tanzania 15
Taylor, Charles 149
Terra Lliure (Catalan nationalist organization) 45
Thrasymachus 113
tipping model 35–6, 43, 58, 77
  and economic payoffs 53–5
  and language 37–9
  marginal groups 50–1
  and national identities 36–40
Toft, Monica 141
translation 33–4, 109
Treaty of Trianon 5
triadic configuration (concept of Rogers Brubaker) 2, 5
trust 108

Uganda 110
Ukraine 15, 16, 23

Ullian, J. S. 144
United Kingdom 4, 32
  colonial rule 76
  Wales 94, 113
United States 81, 111, 127, 132
  African-Americans 7–8, 55
  California 125
  Hopi 70
  Russian speakers 96

van Parijs, Philippe 148
Varshney, Ashutosh 11, 140
Vilar, Pierre 146
violence:
  in Africa 10–11
  civil war 15–18, 21–2, 26, 133
  data 10–11
  ethnic 18–21
  in India 7, 8–9, 11
  intra-group 26
  and nationalism 2–9
Vives, Jaime Vicens 146

Wacziarg, Romain 147
Weber, Eugen 142, 146
Weber, Max 68, 70, 74, 141, 145
Weber, Shlomo 147
Weiner, Myron 139
Weingast, Barry 134, 144, 150
Weinstein, Jeremy 148
Weinstock, Daniel M. 149
Whorf, Benjamin Lee 61, 62, 70, 145
Wilkinson, Steven I. 11, 140
Wilson, Woodrow (American President) 29, 81, 126
World War I 1, 3
World War II 1

Yugoslavia vii